Research Way

Dr. Irfankhan Makrani

DEDICATION

This book is an introduction to the field of research methodology. The goals are to provide a foundation for further study, to stimulate enthusiasm for this important and provocative area, and to promote interest in the primary sources on which this secondary one is based. I have tried to achieve these objectives in the Following ways: This book is an asset for all scholars, students, more people as well as use. Help for new way of research Methods, Concept, Idea of research way

CONTENTS

ACKNOWLEDGMENTS

The author of this book. Dr. Irfankhan Gulamnabi Makrani. He is lecturer (professor) in Department of psychology from Government arts and commerce college Jadar Sabarkantha (North Gujarat). PG Lecture in Psychology in Idar College. He also best 6 research paper publishing and research Generals every 2 month Publish My research paper and 3Books also publish on Psychology Subject related. Really Dr. Irfankhan is very good person and so hard-worker, honest to his duty. He is complete PGDCP-Post graduate diploma guidance and counseling and may be help any guide in problem help students

1   HOW TO WRITE A RESEARCH PROPOSAL

Introduction:

The research proposal is used to assess the originality or quality of the ideas and research feasibility. The research proposal can be prepared around 3500 to 5000 words. Structure of Research Proposal Structure of Research Proposal Title Statement of the research topic Write summary of the identified research topic by considering new, present and pertinent viewpoints of the topic. Remember, most imperative part of a research proposal is clarity on the research topic.

The topic must be explored through appropriate and substantial methods and for which research material is accessible.

The greatest challenge lies in narrowing the topic down. The challenge frequently happens with topics that are still moderately unfamiliar.

Review of Literature:

Write a short and exact overview about the current state of research that is quickly associated with the own research and specify the name the most critical commitments of different researchers.

The proposal has to contain unmistakable and sensible discussion of the theoretical scope or of the framework of thoughts that will be utilized to back the research. The proposal has to demonstrate that you are completely acquainted with the ideas you are managing and that you get a handle on their methodological implications.

Research objectives provide a compact and clear outline of the academic objectives that you need to accomplish through the research. The proposal has to show why expected research is vital and to legitimize the exertion of doing the research.

Scope of the research

Cite by quoting another person word for word (direct quotation). It doesn't matter whether it is a phrase, sentence or paragraph, you will need to provide a reference to the source .cite by paraphrasing or summarizing ideas or data obtained from another source .Use statistics in your work obtained from another source (e.g. population, results of surveys).Use tables, figures, diagrams or images created by someone else Use controversial facts, opinions, or dates from another source. The extent of the study alludes to the parameters under which the review will work. The problem we try to determine will fit with specific parameters.

Methodology

Expected results and output of the study definitely, we don't have results about at the proposal stage. However, we should have some knowledge regarding what sort of information you will gather, and what methodology will be utilized as a part of request to answer the research question or test you theory/hypothesis. It is imperative to persuade the reader of the potential effect of the proposed research. It is compulsory to convey a sense of eagerness and certainty without overstating the benefits of the proposal.

References

Common flaws in proposal writing Failing to provide exact context, Failing to determine the boundary conditions of the research, Failing to theoretical and empirical contributions of the other researchers, Deviating from the proposed idea, Failing to develop coherent and persuasive argument for the proposed research, Failing to follow proper APA style, Failing to structure the proposal in order.

2 HOW TO WRITE A THESIS?

1. First you have to analyze your primary sources. Look for tension, interest, ambiguity, controversy, and/or complication. Once you have a working thesis, you write it down. There is nothing as frustrating as hitting on a great idea for a thesis, then forgetting it when you lose concentration. And by writing down your thesis you will be forced to think of it clearly, logically and concisely. You probably will not be able to write out a final-draft version of your thesis the first time you try, but you'll get yourselves on the right track by writing down what you have.

2. Keep your thesis prominent in your introduction. A good, standard place for your thesis statement is at the end of an introductory paragraph, especially in shorter (5-15 page) essays. Readers are used to finding thesis there, so they automatically pay more attention when they read the last sentence of your introduction. Although this is not required in all academic essays, it is a good rule of thumb

3. Anticipate the counterarguments. Once you have a working thesis, you should think about what might be said against it. This will help you to refine your thesis, and it will also make you think of the arguments that you'll need to refute later on in your essay. Every argument has a counterargument. If yours doesn't, then it's not an argument it may be a fact, or an opinion, but it is not an argument. A thesis is never a question. A thesis is never a list. A thesis should never be vague, combative or confrontational. An ineffective thesis would spark a defensive reaction from readers sympathetic to communism. If readers strongly disagree with you right off the bat, they may stop reading

4. Effective thesis has a definable, arguable claim. Thesis makes a definite, arguable claim. A thesis should be as clear and specific as possible. Avoid overused, general terms and abstractions.

Point

1. Pick a topic that you are interested in. You will be having a lot of research and experimentation ahead of you. It helps to produce good science if you have enthusiasm in what you are doing. Find a broad topic and do a little preliminary work, perhaps making a shortlist of possible areas of like

2. Realistic. If you have difficulty with transport then there is no point picking a project in some far-flung, inaccessible area. You may have to go back to re-sample or clarify your data. For a field study that requires lots of walking or climbing you need to be reasonably fit. If you are not very good at approaching strangers then avoid a subject that requires you to ask people to fill in questionnaires. Play according to your strengths and avoid your weaknesses.

3. Pick a type of research that interests you. Some people might enjoy working in a lab, others sampling in the field. There is no point picking a project with lots of statistical analyses if you hate doing calculations. If you hate book research then try and pick a subject that does not need much.

4. With the above in mind, check out the facilities your department offers. For example, some departments offer help with statistics or using computer programs.

5. Take into account the amount of time and resources you have. It is better to pick a focused topic and be thorough than to try and perform some complex experiment that you struggle to finish. Your topic must be broad enough to ensure that you have enough data but narrow enough to maximize your time and resources.

6. Whilst this is very much a personal decision, sometimes it is better to try and make sure that you think you can work with your supervisor.

7. Sometimes departments have a list of suggested topics; if any of these interest you then talk to the named supervisor and see what it entails.

8. Try and be a little different; if a large number of students research the same topics then there could be a lot of people fighting over one copy of a book or journal.

9. For some areas of research you may need to ask the help of friends to take samples. An example is psychology where you need to entice people to answer your questions or perform your tests. What

measures will you need to entice people? Asking favours, bribery or threats? Try to ensure that you have thought about this before you start.

Remember that people are there to help you. If you not sure of where to start, often the most difficult part, do not be afraid to ask questions from those more knowledgeable in the subject. It is common to feel a little nervous and overwhelmed before starting on a long project but that will pass. Remember that the reputation of your supervisor and department is judged by how you'll perform in your research paper so they will try their Best to guide you.

3 HOW TO PUBLISH A RESEARCH ARTICLE?

Introduction -

For research scholars doing PhD it is mandatory to publish their research papers at international level journals. Many of the students who apply for further studies in technical courses will discover that relevant published research papers benefit during admission process.

1. Preliminary the first activity for publishing a technical paper is to figure out your technical area of interest. Make sure that you have carried out enough studies on basics of that topic. Then you have to update yourselves with the on-going technical happenings in your chosen field. You can do this by

   (A) Reading a lot of technical papers.
       There are a lot of journals and IEEE papers floating around in net.
   (B) Go to one or more conferences, listen carefully to the best talks, and find out what people are thinking about.

2. Read existing Papers Read everything that might be relevant gives you different perspective of the focused topic. But be selective too, for not getting to much deviated from you topic of interest. Getting used to simulation software is much useful for simulating your work. You can find a lot of time during the days and utilize those holidays and free days.

3. A jump start When you first start reading up on a new field, ask your fellow researcher about the most useful journals and conference proceedings in that field and ask for a list of important papers that you are ought to read. This activity will give you a jump start.

4. Crack the jargons and terms one of the tough nuts to crack is capable of understanding the paper published by others. The easiest way is to read it many times. The more times you read the more will be revealed to you. Keep the Internet handy so that you can crack the jargons and terms, which you may find strange.

5. Write down your studies Write down speculations, interesting problems, possible solutions, random ideas, references to look up, notes on papers you've read, outlines of papers to write and interesting quotes. Read back through it periodically. Keeping a journal of your research activities and ideas is very useful.

6. Bits and pieces together now you can identify important open problems in your   research field and also you will be very much aware of what you are doing and what you have to do. The more you go, you'll notice that the bits of random thoughts start to come together and form a pattern, which may be a bright enough for a good paper.

7. Simulation of software Please doesn't pick overly ambitious topics; instead identify a realistic size problem. Gather the Mat lab files available in the Internet that is related to your topic and simulate it for the claimed results Please don't expect the M files readily available for a solution published in a paper. But you can make it of your own by modifying and adding. Once you are able to get the simulated outputs of your solution, you can carry on for making a paper out of it.

8. Essence of your work the essence of your work can be diagnosed by analyzing below listed points. You can increase the maturity of the paper by improving these.

    Significance: Why was this work done? Did you solve an important problem of current interest or is it an obscure or obsolete problem?

    Originality/Novelty: Is your approach novel or is it tried-and- true? Did you need to develop new tools, either analytical or physical?

Completeness: Have you tested a wide range of scenarios, or is this just a simple proof-of-concept? Correct: Is your solution technically sound or are there errors?
Consider improving the same.

9. Anatomy of Paper Generally a paper has seven sections and a maximum of four pages. They are

    1. Abstract,
    2. Introduction,
    3. Existing techniques
    4. Your contribution.
    5. Results
    6. Conclusion

10. The procedure as a part of your paper publication, you can start documenting the 'existing techniques' from the scrap journal you did during the studies. Here you have to extract what all are the techniques existing as a solution for the particular problem and the pros and cons of those. Next, document the 'introduction' about what is the

4 TIPS OF THESIS WRITING

Writing a thesis is a unique experience and there is no general consensus on what the best way to structure it is. As a postgraduate student, you will probably decide what kind of structure suits your research project best after consultation with your supervisor as well as by reading other thesis of previous postgraduate students in your university library. To some extent all post graduate dissertations are unique; however there are two basic structures that a post graduate dissertation can follow. For PhD students, one possibility is to structure the thesis as a series of journal articles that can be submitted for publication to professional journals in the field. This kind of structure would spare you the effort of having to write the thesis and articles for publication separately, however it is relatively unconventional and you should discuss it first with your supervisor before opting for this method.

A more conventional way of structuring a postgraduate thesis is to write it in the form of a book consisting of chapters. Although the number of chapters used is relative to the specific research project and to the course duration, a thesis organized into chapters would typically look like this:

- ➢ **TITLE PAGE** The Opening page including all the relevant information about the thesis.
- ➢ **ABSTRACT** A brief project summary including background, methodology and findings.
- ➢ **CONTENTS** A list of the chapters and figures contained in your thesis.4. **CHAPTER 1** BACKGROUND a description of the rationale behind your project.
  CHAPTER 2 LITERATURE REVIER
  > A more conventional way of structuring a postgraduate thesis is to write it in the form of a book consisting of chapters. Although the number of chapters used is relative to the specific research project and to the course duration, a thesis organized into chapters would typically look like this:

CHAPTER 3 - METHODOLOGY a description of methodology used in your research.

CHAPTER 4-6 DATA ANALYSIS a description of technique used in analyzing your research data.

CHAPTER 7 – DISCUSSION Main conclusions based on the data analysis.

BIBLIOGRAPHY A list of the references cited in your thesis.

APPENDICES Additional materials used in your research. When you start writing your thesis/dissertation depends on the scope of the research project you are describing and on the duration of your course. In some cases, your research project may be relatively short and you may not be able to write much of your thesis before completing the project. However in other instances your project may be relatively long, especially if you are doing a PhD, and you will need to keep writing the thesis while conducting your research. But regardless of the nature of your research project and of the scope of your course, you should start writing your thesis or at least some of its sections as early as possible, and there are a number of good reasons for this:

1. The best way of improving your writing skills is to finish the first draft of your thesis as early as possible and send it to your supervisor for revision. Your supervisor will correct your draft and point out any writing errors. This process will be repeated a few times which will help you recognize and correct writing mistakes yourself as time progresses.

2. If you are not a native English speaker, it may be useful to ask your English friends to read a part of your thesis and warn you about any recurring writing mistakes. Read your section on English language support for more advice.

3. Most universities have writing centers that offer writing courses and other kinds of support for postgraduate students. Attending these courses may help you improve your writing and meet other postgraduate students with whom you will be able to discuss what constitutes a well-written thesis.4. Reading academic articles and searching for various writing resources on the internet will enable you slowly adopt the academic style of writing and eventually you should be able to use it effortlessly when studying for your PhD. The method must be appropriate to fulfilling the overall aims of the study. For example, you need to ensure that you have a large enough sample size to be able to generalize and make recommendations based upon the

findings

5 TIPS OF REFERENCE WRITING

What Is Referencing?

Referencing is a standardized method of formatting the information sources you have used in your assignments or written work. Acknowledge the source, Allows the reader to trace the source As you work on your assignment, you will need to record and keep the details of each source as you use it (this includes details such as author, title, publication date, publisher, place of publication, journal title, volume, issue, page numbers, date viewed or accessed, URL, database, etc.).In-text citations: Both the Harvard AGPS and APA referencing styles used at USQ are author-date styles. The in-text citations will consist mainly of the authors, surnames and author-date styles. The in-text citations will consist mainly of the authors, surnames and the year (and page numbers if appropriate). If there is no discernable author, the title and date are used. Examples can be found in the guides on this site.

List of references. More comprehensive details for each source are put in the list of references at the end of the assignment. This allows the reader to trace and verify your sources. Examples showing the amount of detail required and how to format each source can be found in the guides on this site.

6 PROCEDURES WHY SHOULD I USE REFERENCE?

Shows adherence to academic writing standards. Shows respect for and acknowledge the work of other scholars (thereby avoiding plagiarism).Provides evidence that you have read and considered the relevant literature .Allows validation and confirmation of sources used in your work, and Gives your work credibility.

NEED OF REFERENCING

Cite by quoting another person word for word (direct quotation). It doesn't matter whether it is a phrase, sentence or paragraph, you will need to provide a reference to the source .cite by paraphrasing or summarizing ideas or data obtained from another source .Use statistics in your work obtained from another source (e.g. population, results of surveys).Use tables, figures, diagrams or images created by someone else Use controversial facts, opinions, or dates from another source.

STANDARD REFERENCING STYLES

Harvard APA (American Psychological Association) Bennett, D. R. (2016). An empirical study of industrial consumer buying behaviour: how airlines buy airplanes.

MLA (Modern Language Association of America)

Bennett, D. R. An empirical study of industrial consumer buying behavior: how airlines buy airplanes. (2016).Vancouver Bennett DR. An empirical study of industrial consumer buying behavior: how airlines buy airplanes. Chicago Bennett, D. R. An empirical study of industrial consumer buying behavior: how airlines buy airplanes. (2016).Oxford Ratnagar,S., Trading Encounters: From the Euphrates to the Indus in the Bronze Age , New Delhi, Oxford University Press, 2004.IEEE (Institute of Electrical and Electronics Engineers)B. Klaus and P. Horn, Robot Vision. Cambridge, MA: MIT Press, 1986.

7 RESEARCH METHODOLOGY

Specification – Research Methods:

1. Independent and Dependent Variables
2. Experimental Methods including; Laboratory, Field and Natural Experiments
3. Variables manipulations and control of variables including; independent, dependent, extraneous, confounding, operationalization of variables
4. Aims and Hypotheses, directional, non-directional and null
5. Sampling, the differences between population and sample; sampling techniques including; random, opportunity, volunteer, systematic and stratified; implications of sampling techniques, including bias and generalizability
6. Pilot studies and the aims of piloting
7. Experimental designs; repeated measures, matched pairs, independent groups
8. Observational design; behavioural categories; event sampling; time sampling
9. Questionnaire construction; including the use of open and closed questions
10. Design of interviews
11. Case Studies
12. Control; random allocation, randomisations, standardisation, counterbalancing
13. Demand characteristics and Investigator effects
14. The role of peer review in the scientific process
15. Reliability across all methods of investigation. Ways of assessing reliability: test-retest, inter-observer, improving reliability
16. Types of validity across all methods of investigation; face validity, concurrent validity, ecological validity and temporal validity. Assessment of validity Improving validity.

17. Features of science : objectivity and the empirical method; reliability and falsifiability; theory construction and hypothesis testing; paradigms and paradigm shifts
18. Reporting psychological investigations. Sections of a scientific report; abstract, introduction, methods, results, discussion and referencing
19. Quantitative and qualitative data: the distinction between qualitative and quantitative data collection techniques.
20. Primary and secondary data, including meta-analysis
21. Descriptive statistics: measures of central tendency (mean, median and mode)
22. Measures of dispersion (range and standard deviation)
23. Calculation of percentages
24. Correlational analysis: positive, negative and zero correlations
25. Presentation and display of quantitative data: graphs, tables, scatter grams and bar charts
26. Distributions: normal and skewed distributions: characteristics of normal and skewed distributions
27. Introduction to statistical testing: the sign test
28. Probability and significance: use of statistical tables and critical values in interpretation of significance; Type 1 and Type 2 errors
29. Factors affecting the choice of statistical test, including the level of measurement and experimental design. When to use the following tests: Spearman's Rho, Pearson's R, Wilcoxon T, Mann-Whitney U, related T-tests, unrelated T-Tests and Chi-Squared.
30. Qualitative data analysis; content analysis and thematic analysis

POINT -1 VARIABLE, AIMS AND HYPOTHESES, DIRECTIONAL AND NON-DIRECTIONAL

Variables:

The **independent variable (IV)** is the variable that psychologists **manipulate/change** to see if changing this variable has an effect on the **dependent variable (DV).**

The **dependent variable (DV)** is the variable that the psychologists **measures** (to see if the IV has had an effect).

It is important that the only variable that is changed in research is the **independent variable (IV);** all other variables have to be kept constant across the control condition and the experimental conditions. Only then will researchers be able to observe the true effects of **just** the independent variable (IV) on the dependent variable (DV).

Aims:

An aim is a clear and precise statement of the purpose of the study. It is a statement of why a research study is taking place. This should include what is being studied and what the study is trying to achieve. (e.g. "This study aims to investigate the effects of alcohol on reaction times". It is important that aims created in research are realistic and ethical.

Hypotheses:

This is a testable statement that predicts what the researcher expects to happen in their research. The research study itself is therefore a means of testing whether or not the hypothesis is supported by the findings. If the findings do support the hypothesis then the hypothesis can be retained (i.e., accepted), but if not, then it must be rejected.

Three Different Hypotheses:

(1) **Directional Hypothesis:** states that the IV will have an effect on the DV and what that effect will be (the direction of results). For example, eating smarties will significantly **improve** an individual's dancing ability. When writing a directional hypothesis, it is important that you state exactly **how** the IV will influence the DV.

(2) **Non-Directional Hypothesis:** hypothesis simply states that the IV will have an effect on the DV but **does not predict how** it will affect the results. For example, 'eating smarties will have a significant effect on an individual's dancing ability.'

(3) **A Null Hypothesis:** states that the IV will have no significant effect on the DV, for example, 'eating smarties will have no effect in an individual's dancing ability.'

Exam Tip: One of the questions that you may get asked in the exam is 'when would a psychologist decide to use a **directional hypothesis?'** In general, psychologists use a directional hypothesis when there has been previous research on the topic that they aim to investigate (the psychologist has a good idea of what the outcome of the research is going to be). For example, if a researcher was going to carry research out of the effects of alcohol on reaction times, they would predict a directional hypothesis due to the fact that there has already been lots of research looking at this are.

POINT -2 EXPERIMENTAL METHODS INCLUDING; LABORATORY, FIELD AND NATURAL EXPERIMENTS

Method	Description of Method	Strengths	Weaknesses
Laboratory Experiment	· A highly controlled setting · Artificial setting · High control over the IV and EVs · For example, Loftus and Palmer's study looking at leading questions	(+) High level of control, researchers are able to control the IV and potential EVs. This is strength because researchers are able to establish a cause and effect relationship and there is high internal validity. (+) Due to the high level of control it means that a lab experiment can be replicated in exactly the same way under exactly the same conditions. This is a strength as it means that the reliability of the	(-) Low ecological validity. A lab experiment takes place in an unnatural, artificial setting. As a result participants may behave in an unnatural manner. This is a weakness because it means that the experiment may not be measuring real-life behaviour. (-) Another weakness is that there is a high chance of demand characteristics. For example as the laboratory setting makes participants aware they are taking part in research, this may

research can be assessed (i.e. a reliable study will produce the same findings over and over again).

cause them to change their behaviour in some way. For example, a participant in a memory experiment might deliberately remember less in one experimental condition if they think that is what the experimenter expects them to do to avoid ruining the results. This is a problem because it means that the results do not reflect real-life as they are responding to demand characteristics and not just the independent variable.

Field Experiment

· Real life setting

· Experimenter can control the IV

· Experimenter doesn't have control over EVs (e.g. weather elbow degree of control

(+) High ecological validity.

Due to the fact that a field experiment takes place in a real-life setting, participants are unaware that they are being watched

(-) experiments internal validity and makes a cause and effect relationship difficult to establish.

(-) Difficult to replicate. For

over variables. For example, extraneous variables such as the weather (if a study is taking place outdoors), noise levels or temperature are more difficult to control if the study is taking place outside the laboratory. This is problematic because there is a greater chance of extraneous variables affecting participant's behaviour which reduces the...)

· For example, research looking at altruistic behaviour had a stooge (actor) stage a collapse in a subway and recorded how many passers-by stopped to help.

and therefore are more likely to act naturally. This is the strength because it means that the participant's behaviour will be reflective of their real-life behaviour.

(+) Strength is that there is less chance of demand characteristics. For example, because the research consists of a real life task in a natural environment it's unlikely that participants will change their behaviour in response to demand characteristics. This is positive because it means that the results reflect real-life as they are not responding to demand characteristics, just

example, if a study is taking place outdoors, the weather might change between studies and affect the participants' behaviour. This is a problem because it reduces the chances of the same results being found time and time again and therefore can reduce the reliability of the experiment.

		the independent variable.	

		The **strengths** of the natural experiment are exactly the same as the strengths of the field experiment:	The **weaknesses** of the natural experiment are exactly the same as the strengths of the field experiment:
Natural Experiment	· Real-life setting · Experimenter has no control over EVs or the IV · IV is naturally occurring · For example, looking at the changes in levels of aggression after the introduction of the television. The introduction of the TV is the natural occurring IV and the DV is the changes in aggression (comparing aggression levels before and after the introduction of the TV).	(+) High ecological validity due to the fact that the research is taking place in a natural setting and therefore is reflective of real-life natural behaviour. (+) Low chance of demand characteristics. Because participants do not know that they are taking part in a study they will not change their behaviour and act	(-)Low control over variables. For example, the researcher isn't able to control EVs and the IV is naturally occurring. This means that a cause and effect relationship cannot be established and there is low internal validity. (-) Due to the fact that there is no control over variables, a natural experiment cannot

| unnaturally therefore the experiment can be said to be measuring real-life natural behaviour. | be replicated and therefore reliability is difficult to assess for. |

POINT -3
VARIABLES; MANIPULATIONS AND CONTROL OF VARIABLES INCLUDING; INDEPENDENT, DEPENDENT, EXTRANEOUS, CONFOUNDING, OPERATIONALIZATION OF VARIABLES

Variables:

There are **two main** variables when it comes to psychological research, these are;

(1) **The Independent Variable (IV)** – the variable that is manipulated/changed

(2) **The Dependent Variable – (DV)** the variable that is measured (e.g. it measures whether or not the IV has influence human behaviour).

When carrying out a piece of research, a psychologists main concern is looking at the effects of **just** the IV on the DV, in order to do this, all other extraneous variables (EVs) need to be controlled.

Between the control condition and the experimental condition the only thing that should change is the IV – **for example,** when looking at the effects of music on memory, in the control condition the participants should complete a memory test with **no music playing,** in the experimental condition, the participants should complete a memory test **with music playing.** The only thing that should change across these conditions is whether the participants complete the memory test with or without music. All other variables – the memory test difficulty, age of participant, gender of participant, background noise, temperature of the room etc… should remain consistent.

If a researcher controls for extraneous variables and the only variable to change across the control and experimental condition is the IV it can be seen that the research has been carried out successfully. This means that the researcher has observed the effects of **just** the **IV on the DV,** which also means that the researcher can establish a **cause and effect relationship** (they can be confident that the IV has been the only variable to affect the DV) and therefore can say that their experiment has **high internal validity.** High internal validity is when the researcher is confident that they have measured what they intended to measure (i.e. the effects of just the IV on the DV) and that all extraneous variables (EVs) have been controlled and that there are no confounding variables (CVs) in their study.

Extraneous Variables (EVs): These are variables that researchers do not want in their research. It is important that before a researcher conducts a study they carry out a pilot study to ensure that there are no EVs that could ruin their results. There are four main extraneous variables that you need to know in your exam. It is important that you are able to describe what is meant by these four EVs and that you are able to give examples of each of the four EVs.

The four extraneous variables are:

(1) Participant Variables: This refers to anything specific to the participant that could affect the results of the research, **for example,** a participant's age, gender, intelligence, personality etc…

(2) Demand Characteristics: This refers to environmental clues and cues in an investigation that causes participants to behave unnaturally. Participants respond in one of the following ways:

> A. Attempt to please the experimenter
> B. Attempt to ruin the results ('screw you' effect)
> C. Become more self-conscious

(3) Situational Variables: Refers to the experimental setting and surrounding environment must be controlled between conditions to avoid them impacting on the results, **for example,** the temperature of the room in which the experiment is taking place, the time of day, the weather etc.

(4) Experimenter Effects: This refers to anything specific to the experimenter that could affect the results of the research, **for example,** the gender of the experimenter (e.g. if an experiment was taking place investigating the social life of university students a 50+ researcher may not be the best person to obtain this information from the participants as the participants may feel this person would judge their behaviours – this could lead to the participants not being honest). The mood and personality of the researcher could also be experimenter effects that could impact on the results of the study.

It is important that the researcher plans their research carefully in order to remove any potential extraneous variables (EV). If an EV isn't controlled and interferes with a study this would prevent the researcher from establishing a **cause and effect relationship** and would lead the study to having **low internal validity** – the researcher will not be able to conclude that the IV is the only variable to effect the DV as an EV has been present in the study.

When a study is carried out with an extraneous variable (EV) present, this EV becomes a **confounding variable (CV)** due to the fact that its presence confounds the results of the study.

Operationalizing Independent Variables (IVs) and Dependent Variables (DVs):

In experiments, the researcher manipulates the IV to find the effect it has on the DV. To preserve the internal validity of an experiment, the IV and DV must be operationalized.

Operationalization means defining the variables (both the independent variable (IV) and the dependent variable (DV)) in such a way that they can be precisely tested and measured. More simply, operationalizing variables means **stating** how the IV and the DV **have been measured.** The process of operationalizing variables allows other researchers to **replicate** previous research studies precisely.

For example, if a researcher was looking at the effects of hunger on memory, they would have to consider how they are going to measure the IV 'hunger' and how they are going to measure the DV 'memory.'

There are a number of ways in which **hunger can be operationalized/measured:**

(1) a questionnaire assessing hunger, the higher the score on the questionnaire could indicate a high level of hunger

(2) the amount of ghrelin present in the participant's stomach – a high amount of ghrelin indicates that the participant is hungry

(3) The amount of time passed since the person last ate (assuming that the more time that has passed since a person's last meal the hungrier they are).

THERE ARE A NUMBER OF WAYS IN WHICH **MEMORY CAN BE OPERATIONALIZED/MEASURED** THE MOST POPULAR METHOD WOULD BE GIVING THE PARTICIPANTS A MEMORY TESTS AND OBSERVING THE SCORE THAT THE PARTICIPANTS OBTAIN ON THIS TEST.

POINT -4
VARIABLES, AIMS AND HYPOTHESES, DIRECTIONAL AND NON-DIRECTIONAL

Variables:

The **independent variable (IV)** is the variable that psychologists **manipulate/change** to see if changing this variable has an effect on the **dependent variable (DV).**

The **dependent variable (DV)** is the variable that the psychologists **measures** (to see if the IV has had an effect).

It is important that the only variable that is changed in research is the **independent variable (IV);** all other variables have to be kept constant across the control condition and the experimental conditions. Only then will researchers be able to observe the true effects of **just** the independent variable (IV) on the dependent variable (DV).

Aims:

An aim is a clear and precise statement of the purpose of the study. It is a statement of why a research study is taking place. This should include what is being studied and what the study is trying to achieve. (e.g. "This study aims to investigate the effects of alcohol on reaction times".

It is important that aims created in research are realistic and ethical.

Hypotheses:

This is a testable statement that predicts what the researcher expects to happen in their research. The research study itself is therefore a means of testing whether or not the hypothesis is supported by the findings. If the findings do support the hypothesis then the hypothesis can be retained (i.e., accepted), but if not, then it must be rejected.

Three Different Hypotheses:

(1) **Directional Hypothesis:** states that the IV will have an effect on the DV and what that effect will be (the direction of results). For example, eating smarties will significantly **improve** an individual's dancing ability. When writing a directional hypothesis, it is important that you state exactly **how** the IV will influence the DV.

(2) **Non-Directional Hypothesis:** hypothesis simply states that the IV will have an effect on the DV but **does not predict how** it will affect the results. For example, 'eating smarties will have a significant effect on an individual's dancing ability.'

(3) **A Null Hypothesis:** states that the IV will have no significant effect on the DV, for example, 'eating smarties will have no effect in an individual's dancing ability.'

Exam Tip: One of the questions that you may get asked in the exam is 'when would a psychologist decide to use a **directional hypothesis?'** In general, psychologists use a directional hypothesis when there has been previous research on the topic that they aim to investigate (the psychologist has a good idea of what the outcome of the research is going to be). For example, if a researcher was going to carry research out of the effects of alcohol on reaction times, they would predict a directional hypothesis due to the fact that there has already been lots of research looking at this area.

POINT 6 PILOT STUDIES

Pilot study: This is a small-scale version (dry run) of the real research often carried out before the full-scale research project begins. Based on a small sample, they are usually quick, easy to conduct and inexpensive. They are used to check the research works as it is intended to, does not have any confounding variables and is practical.

The main reason why pilot studies are conducted is to check the following:

(1) Are there any demand characteristics in the study? Is so, the researcher will need to remove these before the full study in order to increase internal validity.

(2) Are the instructions clear? It is important that the instructions of the experiment are clear that way participants are fully informed about what they are expected to do as part of the experiments. Unclear instructions could lead to participants responding at random in the experiment which could lead to inaccurate results.

(3) Are the resources adequate? For example, when carrying out an observation, a pilot study can allow the researcher to check that their behaviour schedule/tally chart is adequate and that no behaviours have been missed off the chart.

(4) (4) Are there any EVs (extraneous variables) that could affect the results? A pilot study will allow a researcher to identify the EVs in their study and will allow them to assess what control strategies they need to put in place before they carry out the real study.

POINT -7 EXPERIMENTAL DESIGNS

An experimental design is the way in which the participants are used across the different conditions in a laboratory experiment. In a laboratory experiment there is always one control condition (this is a group of participants matched as closely as possible to the experimental group that don't receive the IV. They act as a baseline to compare against the experimental group), along with one or more experimental conditions.

Researchers have to decide whether or not they want to use the same or different participants in the control and the experimental condition.

There are **three experimental designs** that a researcher can use.

(1) **Independent Measures** – this is when a researcher uses participants once in either the control condition or the experimental condition.

(2)**Repeated Measures** – this is when participants are used in each condition, both the control condition and the experimental condition(s).

(3)**Matched Pairs** – this is when participants take part in only one condition (either the control or the experimental condition), however, participants are matched in terms of certain characteristics that may affect the outcome of the study, (for example, in a study looking at memory performance, participants across the control and the experimental condition could be matched in terms of age due to the fact that age can have an effect on memory performance).

Exam Tip: In the exam, you need to be able to outline each experimental design in terms of how the participants are used, in addition, you also need to be able to look at a description of research and suggest what experimental design a researcher would be best using. The best way to justify the choice of experimental design is to know **two** strengths and **two** weaknesses of each design.

Evaluation of the 3 Experimental Designs:

Revising the evaluation of the three experimental designs can be made easy by learning the following items and by being able to apply these items as either a strength or weakness for each of the designs.

(1) **The number of participants required for a study** (the less participants required in a study the better. It can be quite difficult for researchers to obtain participants for their study especially if funding is limited and the researcher is unable to pay the participants for taking part in their research). **This can be seen to be strength of the repeated measures design –**

fewer participants are needed as each participant takes place in both the control and the experimental condition. However, **this can be seen to be a weakness of the independent measures design** as participants only takes part in one condition meaning that twice as many participants are needed to take part in a study where there is a control and experimental condition.

(2) **Participant variables** – everybody is unique and different. Remember; when conducting research, the experimenter wants the only differences between the experimental and control condition to be the manipulation of the independent variable. If we use different participants in the control and experimental condition, not only is the IV different across these two conditions, a potential extraneous variable (EV) is introduced in that there are **participant differences.** Research is better when there are no individual differences, therefore strength of the **repeated measures design** is that the same participants are used in each condition and therefore there are no participant variables. However, when using a design like the **independent measures design,** participant variables are created which may lower a study's internal validity.

(3) **Demand characteristics:** are when participants pick up on clues and cues in the experiment which help them to guess what the research is about and predict what the experimenter is looking for. When participants pick up on such clues and cues they often change the way they would naturally behave – they act in a way that will give the experimenter what they want so that they appear 'normal,' or they may deliberately act in a way that is different to what the experimenter is looking for to avoid being a conformist. Again, demand characteristics are an extraneous/confounding variable that experimenters do not want in their study (remember, the experimenter is looking to observe the effects of just the IV on the DV). A weakness of the **repeated measures design** is that it can create demand characteristics (participants taking part in each condition can help them to guess the aim of the study). Strength of the **independent measures design** is that participants only

take part in one condition therefore demands characteristics are minimised.

(4) **Order effects:** When participants repeat a task, results can be affected by order effects. Order effects include:

- Performing less well than you would normally due to boredom or fatigue
- Performance improving through practice in the first condition

Strength of the independent measures design is that because participants only take part in **one condition** participants are less likely to become border or practiced and therefore the experiment is more likely to measure natural real-life behaviour. On the other hand, a weakness of the repeated measures design is that because participants take part in **all the conditions** in the research they are more likely to become bored or practiced as they progress through the conditions which will result in measuring unnatural behaviour thus lowering internal validity.

Independent Measures	Repeated Measures	Matched Pairs
(+) Reduces the chances of demand characteristics because participants only take part in one condition they are less likely to pick up on clues and cues in the experiment which could lead to participants changing their behaviour in order to please the experimenter. **This is strength because** it means that the experiment will have	(+) Fewer participants are required because the same participants are used in all of the conditions. This means that less money is spent. (+) Participant variable are eliminated as the same participants are being used in each condition. This means	(+) Reduces the chances of demand characteristics because participants only take part in one condition they are less likely to pick up on clues and cues in the experiment which could lead to participants changing their behaviour in order to please the experimenter. **This is strength because** it means that the experiment will have

high internal validity and will measure what it intends to.

that participant variables are kept consistent, providing all other EVs are controlled this means that the only variable to change across the different conditions is the IV which means that a cause and effect relationship can be established.

high internal validity and will measure what it intends to.

(+) Reduces the chances of order effects. Because participants are only tested in one condition so they will not improve through practise or become bored through repetition. **This is strength because** it means that the experiment will have high internal validity and therefore is measuring what it intends to.

(+) Reduces the chances of order effects. Because participants are only tested in one condition so they will not improve through practise or become bored through repetition. **This is strength because** it means that the experiment will have high internal validity and therefore is measuring what it intends to.

(-) Requires twice the number of participants needed by a repeated measures design which is a weakness because it could make the research more expensive to carry out.

(-) Increases the chances of order effects as participants take part in **all the conditions** the research therefore they are more likely to become bored or practiced as they progress through the conditions which will result in measuring unnatural behaviour thus lowering internal validity.

(-) Requires twice the number of participants needed by a repeated measures design which is a weakness because it could make the research more expensive to carry out.

(-) High chance of participant variables as different participants is being used in each condition. This means that the IV isn't the only

(-)A weakness of

(-) High chance of participant variables as different participants is being used in each condition. This means that the IV isn't the only variable to change across the different conditions and therefore a cause and effect relationship cannot be established.

the **repeated measures design** is that it can create demand characteristics, participants taking part in each condition can help them to guess the aim of the study and therefore change their behaviour.

variable to change across the different conditions and therefore a cause and effect relationship cannot be est.

POINT-7 OBSERVATIONAL DESIGN; BEHAVIOURAL CATEGORIES; EVENT SAMPLING; TIME SAMPLING

Observations (Naturalistic)

Description:

This refers to the observation of behaviour in its natural setting. The researcher makes no attempt to influence the behaviour of those being observed or manipulate variables. The aim of the research is to observe naturally occurring behaviour.

(1) **Disclosed/Overt Observation** Participants are aware they're part of an observation.

(+) Strength of this type of observation is that participants can give consent – therefore this type of observation can be seen to be ethical.

(-) A weakness of this type of observation is that participants know that they are being watched and therefore may change their behaviour to suit the experimenter (respond with demand characteristics).

(2) **Undisclosed/Covert Observation** Participants are not aware they are part of an observation.

(+) Participants are unaware that they are being watched therefore, any behaviour observed will be naturally occurring.

(-) Limited to public places (where people expect to be observed) therefore there is a limit to what behaviour can be observed. (-)
Undisclosed observations can be argued to be unethical however; researchers believe that as long as only public behaviour is being observed then this type of observation can be deemed to be ethical.

Other observation types:

(1) Participant Observation: Involves the observer becoming actively involved in the activities of the people being studied. Participant observation can be either disclosed (people are told they are being observed) or undisclosed (participant is unaware of being observed).

(2) Non-participant Observation: Non-participant involves the researcher observing the behaviour from a distance; they do not become actively involved in the behaviour to be studies.

Designing a Naturalistic Observation

Remember that observations are not experiments and so there is no IV, instead behaviour is studies in the environment in which it would typically be seen.

You need to decide on the following things;

- Aim
- Hypothesis
- Sample
- Type of data
- How data will be recorded

Types of sampling within an observation (ways of collecting data):

(1) Event sampling:

- Involves counting the number of times that certain behaviours (event) occurs while observing an individual, using a behaviour schedule (quantitative data) A behavioural schedule is like a tally chart/a list of behaviours, every time a behaviour is observed a 'tally' is placed next to that behaviour.

(+) This is useful if you have a lot of behaviours you need to record

(-) However, it does lack details (e.g. no information about preceding events)

(2) Time sampling

This means recording behaviours in a given time frame. I.e. you might record what the participant does every 60 seconds.

(+) This is useful if you have a lot of behaviours you need to record

(-) This means that not every behaviour is noted and so the end data can lack detail

Creating and using a behaviour schedule

1) Identify a list of behaviours (categories/events) that you would expect from the observation (e.g. observing in a day care might include sharing, shouting, crying etc.).

Aggressive Behaviour	Tally	Frequencies
Kicking		
Smacking		
Punching		
Biting		

2) Conduct a pilot study to ensure that behaviours have not been omitted from your behaviour schedule

3) Create a final list of behaviours (categories/events)

4) Complete the observation tallying whenever one of the categories is observed

Note: the categories must be objective and operationalized (measurable), cover all potential behaviours and be mutually exclusive (the observer should not have to mark 2 categories with one behaviour).

Reliability and Validity in Observations

Reliability: The data produced from an observation can be very subjective- for example, one observer might tick that behaviour has occurred while another observer might not, making the observation unreliable.

How can reliability be improved? Inter-ratter/observer reliability – to use the same behaviour schedule and to ask at least two observers to rate (or code) the behaviours viewed (the observation could be videotaped to make this easier). A correlational analysis is then completed on the results (to test for consistency between the observer's results) and if there is a significant correlation, then the observation is said to be reliable (i.e., there is inter-ratter/observer reliability). One way to objectively assess for inter-ratter reliability is to carry out a statistical test (Spearman's Rho or Pearson's R).

Validity: Ecological validity is likely to be high in a naturalistic observation because it involves studying natural behaviours in a natural environment (however, a natural setting does not guarantee high ecological validity – participants behaviour could be affected by the presence of the researcher).

Internal validity may be at risk if the coding system (behaviour schedule) is flawed. E.g. if an observer has to make an interpretation about a behaviour before coding it, then the behaviour may not be accurately recorded. The validity can also be affected by observer bias – what someone observes can be influenced by their expectations.

Observations:

Strengths:

(1) **POINT:** Strength of naturalistic observations is that they can hold high ecological validity.
EXAMPLE: For example, an observation of children's playing behaviour in the school playground is representative of their real-life behaviour. **EVALUATION:** This is strength because participants tend to behave naturally and results can usually be generalised to other real-life settings.

(2) **POINT:** Strength of naturalistic observations is that they can have low demand characteristics when an undisclosed observation is used.
EXAMPLE: For example, children covertly observed playing in the playground will behave naturally as they are not aware that they are being closely watched by an adult.

EVALUATION:

This is positive because the findings will represent their real-life behaviour.

Weaknesses:

(1) **POINT:** A weaknesses associated with naturalistic observations is that they lack control.

EXAMPLE: For example, potential EVs could interfere with the behaviour of the participant, children being observed playing in a playground may behave differently depending on the temperature outdoors.

EVALUATION: is problematic because observed behaviour might have occurred due to these uncontrolled variables and therefore a result cause and effect relationship cannot be established.

(2) **POINT:** A weakness of naturalistic observations is that they can be affected by observer bias.

EXAMPLE: For example, observers have to interpret what they see and this can be affected by bias, such as if a researcher has predicted that boys will be more aggressive than girls, they may only report the behaviour that fits in with these expectations.

EVALUATION: This is a problem because if researchers are selective in what they notice in this way, their findings are no longer reflective of the truth.

POINT -8 QUESTIONNAIRE CONSTRUCTIONS; INCLUDING THE USE OF OPEN AND CLOSED QUESTIONS

Self-Report Methods – Questionnaires

A questionnaire is a set of written questions on a topic on which opinions are sought. Questionnaires are frequently used in survey research in which information is gathered regarding people's attitudes and beliefs.

Designing questionnaires – question choice

Closed Questions (fixed choice):

These have specific, limited answers. Often a statement is given to the respondent and they must choose from several fixed responses. The following example is often referred to as a Likert Scale.

Example: Members of the Royal Family should not receive money that has been raised from the people's taxes.

Strongly Agree Agree Undecided Disagree   Strongly Disagree

5   4   3   2   1

This kind of question would collect quantitative data.

Evaluation of using Closed Questions in Research

Strengths:

(1) **POINT:** Strength of using closed questions in research is the fact that they will collect quantitative data.

EXAMPLE: For example, that encourage participants to circle options (e.g. circle from the list the symptoms of depression you have suffered from over the last 12 months) allows researchers to calculate frequencies and averages. **EVALUATION:** This is strength because it means that the researcher can statistically analyse the data, produce graphs allowing for a thorough numerical analysis to be completed on the data.

(3) **POINT:** Strength of using closed questions in research is that it is easy to replicate the study. This means that since the questions are standardised it is easy to replicate the questionnaire.

EXAMPLE: For example, the same questionnaire can be administered over and over again and the results of this can be compared.

EVALUATION: This is positive because it allows for the questionnaires to be assessed in terms of their reliability.

Weaknesses:

(1) **POINT:** A weakness of using closed questions in research is that they obtain quantitative data.

EXAMPLE: For example, participant responses will be summarised in numerical form and therefore may lack detail and depth (e.g. participants are not given the option to elaborate/fully explain their responses.

EVALUATION: This is a weakness because the data can be criticised for not accurately representing the complexity of human behaviour.

2 **POINT:** Another weakness of using closed questions and questionnaires is that participants may respond in a socially desirable way. This means that participants may give a response they think portrays them in the best possible way.

EXAMPLE: For example, participants may answer sensitive questions about their weight or sexual activity falsely in order to portray a more desirable image of them.

EVALUATION: This is problematic because it means the findings are not representative of the truth.

Open Questions

With this type of question the respondent is given a high level of freedom with their answers. Often the researcher simply asks a question and provides space underneath for the respondent to write their answer.

Example: What is your opinion about the Royal family receiving money from the taxpayer?

This type of question would collect qualitative data.

Using Open Questions in Research

Strengths:

(1) **POINT:** Strength of using a set of open questions is that these types of questions collect qualitative data.

EXAMPLE: For example, open questions allow participants to expand on their answers and provide lots of detail about their behaviour.

EVALUATION: This is strength because open questions collect rich qualitative data which helps researchers develop a better, more in depth knowledge of human behaviour.

(2) **POINT:** Strength of using open questionnaires in research is that it is easy to replicate the study. This means that since the questions are standardised it is easy to replicate the questionnaire.

EXAMPLE: For example, the same questionnaire can be administered over and over again and the results of this can be compared.

EVALUATION: This is positive because it allows for the questionnaires to be assessed in terms of their reliability.

Weaknesses:

(1) **POINT:** A weakness of using open questions in research is that the data collected is in qualitative form.

EXAMPLE: For example, open questions allow the participants to fully explain their behaviour in lots of detail.

EVALUATION: This is a weakness because when the researcher comes to analysing the data it is very difficult for them to carry out any statistical tests which means that it can be difficult to draw any firm conclusions on the basis of using inferential statistics.

(2) **POINT:** Another weakness of using open questions and questionnaires is that participants may respond in a socially desirable way. This means that participants may give a response they think portrays them in the best possible way.

EXAMPLE: For example, participants may answer sensitive questions about their weight or sexual activity falsely in order to portray a more desirable image of them.

EVALUATION: This is problematic because it means the findings are not representative of the truth.

Designing questionnaires (self-report methods) – administering the questionnaire

(1) **Postal questionnaires:** This involves sending out questionnaires to people through the post. **However,** this could cause an unrepresentative sample because only people who have time will respond to the questionnaires, this may exclude people who work, have or have full time family commitments.

(2) **Magazine and newspaper questionnaires:** This involves asking the readers to send in the completed questionnaire. **However,** this could bring about an unrepresentative sample as only readers of that particular magazine will respond to the questionnaire. This will exclude individuals who don't read this magazine.

Designing questionnaires – ambiguity of questions

Designing the questions for your survey is quite an art. In general, your questions must be clear, simple and mean the same thing to all respondents. The latter means that they must not be ambiguous. Even apparently straightforward questions may be misunderstood.

Poorly designed questions could lower the internal validity of an investigation – in order to increase internal validity, it is important that researchers carry out a pilot study in order to ensure that their questions are clear, not ambiguous and can be understood by the participants.

Designing questionnaires (self-report methods) – reliability and validity

Reliability – Reliability can be assessed by giving two or more researchers the same questions to analyse. If there is a high level of agreement between researchers, then the questionnaire is seen as reliable. You could also use test-retest to assess the reliability of a questionnaire.

Validity – There is a risk that participants responding to a questionnaire will not do so honestly. Consider the following questions- 1. What is your current weight? 2. Have you ever driven whilst drunk? **In these types of questions,** due to the fact that they are socially sensitive, participants are more likely to lie/give false information.

If people don't respond in an honest way then the questionnaire is not measuring what it intends to measure accurately. This means that it will lack internal validity.

Self-Report Methods/Questionnaires:

Strengths:

(1) **POINT:** Strength of closed questionnaires is that they collect quantitative data. This means that questionnaires often collect quantitative data (particularly when closed questions are used).

EXAMPLE: For example, a questionnaire using a likert scale would provide the researcher with numerical data to analyse.

EVALUATION: This is positive because numbers are easy to analyse and compare.

(2) **POINT:** A strenght of closed questionnaires is that they can easily be replicated. This means that since the questions are standardised it is easy to replicate the questionnaire.

EXAMPLE: For example, the same questionnaire can be administered over and over again and the results of this can be compared.

EVALUATION: This is positive because it allows the reliability of the questionnaire to be assessed.

Weaknesses:

(1) **POINT:** A weakness of questionnaires is that they can lead to social desirability. This means that participants may give answers which they think portrays themselves in the best possible way.

EXAMPLE: For example, participants may answer sensitive questions about their weight or sexual activity falsely in order to portray a more desirable image of them.

EVALUATION: This is problematic because it means the findings are not representative of the truth.

(2) **POINT:** A weakness of questionnaires is that ambiguous questions can negatively affect participant responses. This means that sometimes questions may be open to different interpretations.

EXAMPLE: For example, one respondent might interpret the same question differently to another respondent.

EVALUATION: This is a problem because it means that respondents' answers are not directly comparable and this compromises the internal validity of the findings.

POINT -9 DESIGN OF INTERVIEWS

Self-Report Methods – Interviews

Interviews are often more like a conversation. The interviewer has some questions he wishes to ask on a specific topic, but there are no predetermined way of asking questions and no pre-set order in administering them.

Interviews involve researchers asking questions in a face-to face situation. They can be very different but there are two broad types:

(1) **Structured (or formal):** A questionnaire is read to participants and the interviewer writes down their responses.

(2) **Unstructured (or informal):** Less controlled involving an informal discussion on a particular topic (more like a conversation)

Interviews – Structured interviews: The design of structured interviews is similar to the design of questionnaires. The only real difference is the presence of the interviewer. Because of the interviewer's presence, experimenter effects can significantly affect the results. (However, these effects are more pronounced in unstructured interviews).

Interviews – Unstructured Interviews: Unstructured interviews are not standardised. The researcher has several topics to cover, but the questions are not usually pre-set. Unstructured interviews are less formal, more open-ended, and flexible and free flowing than structured interviews. The key to successful unstructured interviews is trust. (Respondent must feel the researcher is sympathetic and interested in their opinion.

Problems that can occur when carrying out interviews:

Experimenter Effects: The personal and social characteristics of the interviewer can affect the respondent's answers. Some researchers suggest matching interviewers and respondents in terms of age, gender, ethnicity and social class on the assumption that they are more likely to "open up" to people that they perceive are similar to themselves.

Demand characteristics: Unstructured interviews are very susceptible to demand characteristics, experimenter/ investigator effects and social desirability effects because of the face-to-face element in this research method.

Reliability: In general, reliability for unstructured interviews is low – two different interviewers may well receive different data from the same participant. Validity in Interviews However, it is argued that their validity is high – because they are more likely to provide rich data and reveal the true meanings which direct behaviour. N.B the same issues apply for questionnaires and structured interviews.

Evaluation of self-report interviews:

Strengths

(1) **POINT:** Strength of using an interview is that it gains the respondents viewpoint. This means opportunities are provided in an interview for respondents to give their own point of view in their own way.

EXAMPLE: For example, in an interview they are able to talk about things which interest them rather than simply responding to pre-set questions in a pre-defined manner.

EVALUATION: This is positive because these more personalised responses can produce new and important insights.

(3) **POINT:** Strength of using interviews is that it produces qualitative data. This means that interviews can produce rich, in-depth and detailed qualitative data.

EXAMPLE: For example, if the respondent feels that the interviewer is sympathetic and understanding towards them, respondents may feel secure enough to provide a great amount of detail about them.

EVALUATION: This is positive because more detail creates a more representative impression of the respondent.

Weaknesses:

(1) **POINT:** A weakness of carrying out an interview is that it collects qualitative data which can be difficult to analyse. This means that it is difficult and time consuming to analyse much of the data that is provided by interviews.

EXAMPLE: For example, in-depth and detailed responses to questions from different respondents are very difficult to compare with one another. **EVALUATION:** This is problematic because it leads to a very time-consuming process of analysis.

(4) **POINT:** A weaknesses of carrying out an interview is that often investigator effects are present. This means that because interviews

involve face to face contact between researcher and participant, the researcher may affect the participant's behaviour.

EXAMPLE: For example, the researcher may unconsciously convey their hypothesis to the participant through their tone of voice or facial expressions. **EVALUATION:** This is a problem as it can have an effect on the way participants behave and answer the questions creating an unrepresentative impression of themselves.

POINT -10 POINT CASE STUDIES

Case Studies

Description of Case Studies:

- An in-depth, detailed investigation of an individual or group.
- It would usually include biographical details, as well as details of behaviours or experiences of interest to the researcher.
- Usually carried out in the real world
- Can use a variety of Psychology research methods (experimental and non-experimental) in order to collect data for the case study.

Methods used to collect information for case studies:

- Questionnaires (open and closed questions)
- Interviews

- Observations

Evaluation of Case Studies:

Strengths:

(1) **POINT:** Strength of a case study is that it produces rich, detailed data. **EXAMPLE:** For example, a case study of an individual's life is incredibly detailed and may highlight a number of important experiences that could have combined to cause them to become mentally ill. **EVALUATION:** This is positive because information that may be overlooked using other methods is likely to be identified.

(2) **POINT:** strength so a cause study is that it provides insight into individuals.

EXAMPLE: For example, rare mental disorders make it impossible to study large amounts of participants with that disorder because the behaviours or experiences are so unique that they could not have been studied in any other way.

EVALUATION: This is positive because it helps to improve our understanding of behaviours that would otherwise not be possible.

Weaknesses:

(1) **POINT:** A weakness of a case study is that it is difficult to generalise the results.
EXAMPLE: For example, a case study of an individual person might not be representative of anyone else because experiences are so individual that another person may not react in the same way.
EVALUATION: This is a problem as it's difficult to generalise to the rest of the population (low population validity) as each case has unique characteristics.

(2) **POINT:** A weakness of a case study is that it collects retrospective data.

EXAMPLE: For example, a researcher might rely on asking individuals about their past to help form the case study, which can be reconstructive.

EVALUATION: This is a problem as such evidence may have been recalled inaccurately and may therefore be unreliable.

POINT -11 VALIDITY

Validity

Validity means accuracy. Results are valid if they accurately show what they are intended to show (.e.g. did you measure what you wanted to? Can you generalize the results?).

You need to know about **internal** and **external** validity.

(1) **Internal validity:** Refers to whether or not the research measured what it intended to measure (e.g. the effects of the IV on the DV) to work out whether a piece of research has high internal validity, ask yourself:

- Were EV's controlled? (Yes)
- Were there any CV's? (No)

- Did the research actually measure the effect of the IV on the DV? (Yes)
- If you find the answers above then the research has high internal validity – this is good because you can establish cause and effect between the IV and the DV. Highly controlled pieces of research have high internal validity.

Ways of Measuring/Assessing Internal Validity

1. **Face validity:** Whether a measure appears, at face value, to test what it claims to. For example, does an interview about addiction to alcohol genuinely measure drinking habits or does it simply elicit socially desirable responses? If it includes questions that trigger socially desirable responses, it is likely to have low internal validity.

2. **Concurrent validity:** Whether a new test produces a similar measure of a variable as existing tests of the same phenomenon. A new questionnaire that identifies risk factors in drug abuse should find many of the same risk factors as an existing, well-known questionnaire if it has high internal validity.

3. **Predictive validity:** Whether the measure can accurately forecast future consequences. For example, a test designed to identify risk factors for alcoholism could be followed up and if validity is high, those identified as having higher risk factors will be more likely to exhibit signs of alcohol abuse.

It is important when conducting research that internal validity is high and that the researchers can be happy that the IV is the only variable affecting the DV (when this is the case, a cause and effect relationship can be established). In order to improve internal validity, researchers adopt a number of different methods.

Strategies to Improve (Increase) Internal Validity:

(1) Standardized Instructions – a set of instructions/script that is followed by a researcher when carrying out a study. These instructions/script indicate to the experimenter how to welcome the participant, how to introduce the study, how to conduct the study and how to end the study/thank the participants. This script ensures that all trials of the researcher are conducted in exactly the same way for each participant.

What EV does this strategy overcome?

- **Experimenter Effects** – due to the fact that the experimenter is following a script, they are less likely to lead the participants to behave in a specific way.
- **Situational Variable** – can also avoid situational variables as usually standardized instructions indicate the experimenter exactly how the research environment should be set up (e.g. temperature of the room, resources etc…) this ensures that the environment is consistent for each participant.

(2) Double-Blind Technique – when the participant is unaware of the true aim of the study that they are taking part in. Further, the key researcher employs a research assistant to carry out the study who is also unaware of the true sims/nature of the experiment that they are conducting.

What EV does this strategy overcome?

- **Demand Characteristics** – participants are less likely to change their behaviour if the true aim of the study is not communicated to them until the end of the research. This leads to participants display more accurate behaviour.
- **Experimenter Effects** – if the research assistant is unaware of the true aims of the research, they will be unable to suggest to the participant how they wish them to behave/less likely to influence participant behaviour.

(3) Single-Blind Technique – when the participant taking part in the study is unaware of the true aims of the research that they are taking part in.

What EV does this strategy overcome?

- **Demand Characteristics** – participants are less likely to change their behaviour if the true aim of the study is not communicated to them until the end of the research. This leads to participants display more accurate behaviour.

(4) Automation – when the instructions of an experiment are recorded and are played to the participants (as oppose to receiving instructions directly from the researcher).

What EV does this strategy overcome?

- **Experimenter Effects** – due to the fact that the researcher doesn't come into contact with the participant (because instructions are given through a pre-recorded tape), the experimenter will be unable to suggest to the participant how they wish them to behave/less likely to influence participant behaviour.

(5) Experimental Designs can also be used to increase internal-validity.

- **Independent Measures Design** – when participants take part in just one condition in a piece of research. **This helps to overcome demand characteristics as participants taking part in only one condition are unlikely to guess the aim of the research and change their behaviour. Also overcomes order effects, participants only taking part in one condition are less likely to become practiced or bored.**

- **Repeated Measures Design** – when participants take place in every condition in a piece of research. **This method would overcome participant variables, because the same participant takes part in each condition there is consistency in relation to participant characteristics (gender, age etc…). This means that (due to the fact participant variables are being controlled) the research is more likely to be measuring just the effects of the IV on the DV.**

- **Matched Pairs Design** – when participants take part in just one condition in a piece of research however, participants in say condition 1, are matched with participants in condition 2 on a certain characteristic (e.g. IQ, age, gender etc…) **This method would overcome participant variables, because the key participant characteristics are matched across the conditions therefore there is consistency in relation to participant characteristics (gender, age etc…). His means that (due to the fact participant variables are being controlled) the research is more likely to be measuring just the effects of the IV on the DV.**

(6) Counter-Balancing- Used when a repeated measures design has been used in research in order to avoid **order effects**. Experimenters fear that when a repeated measures design is used, the result of a piece of research runs the risk of being bias. For example, take an experiment with 2 conditions (condition A and B), if participants complete condition A first followed by condition B last researchers say that performance in condition A is usually reflective of the participants real-life behaviour. In condition B however, because the participants have already completed part of the experiment, it is possible that their behaviour may change in one of two ways;

- **Order Effects** – they may become **practiced** at the task (get better at the research task that they have been asked to do) which could cause participant performance to become unnaturally inflated (therefore not measuring true behaviour).
- **Order Effects** – the participant may become **bored** in the second condition and may not try/give the experiment their true attention which again would mean that condition B is measuring unnatural behaviour.

If a researcher asks that participants always complete condition A followed by B, participant performance may always be unnatural in condition B (i.e. in a memory test, participant performance might look better in condition B because they have been practicing remembering things or may become worse because after completing the memory test in condition A, they now can't be bothered to complete the memory test in condition B). This will lead to bias results and the researcher isn't accurately measuring what they are intending to measure. Adopting the **counter-balancing method** involved half of the participants completing condition a first followed by B, and the other half of the participants completing condition B first followed by B. This means that if there are any order effects, this negative effect will be spread across both conditions (rather just one condition – usually B) which means that the research will have measured more accurately what it intends to measure. Use the phrase ABBA to help you remember this method (50% of participant's complete conditions AB, 50% of participant's complete conditions BA).

(7) Random Allocation – when participants are randomly allocated to either condition A or B. This is done to fairly distribute participant variables. **This overcomes participant variables, ensuring that there is an even split of participant characteristics balanced across all the conditions in the research.**

External Validity

External validity: Refers to whether the research can be generalised outside the research setting to;

- other settings (**ecological**)
- other people (**population**)
- Other times (**temporal**) to work out whether a piece of research has high external validity, ask yourself; has the research been done in a natural setting? (Yes) Is the sample of participant's representative of the entire target population? (Yes) Is the time in which the research was conducted reflective of other periods in time (i.e. is there anything socially significant occurring at the time?) (Yes) If you find the answers above then the research has high external validity – this is good because you can generalise your findings beyond the research setting, sample and time.

Examples of External Validity:

(1) If your experiment uses only men, yet is supposed to represent the whole population (both men and women) then it may be said to have **low population validity**

(2) If you carry out your first experiment in a classroom and find the same results when you repeat it in the canteen your experiment can be said to have **high ecological validity**

(3) If you decide to replicate an experiment that was conducted in 1963 but you find very different results then the original experiment can be said to have **low temporal validity.**

Improving External Validity

As well as controlling extraneous variables to improve internal validity, it is also possible to improve the external validity of your research.

(1) Improving **population validity** – researchers need to make sure that they have conducted their research on a wide, representative sample. The sample in the research needs to include all groups in the target population.

(2) Improving **ecological validity** – researchers need to make sure that they conduct research in a natural, non-artificial environment.

(3) Improving **temporal validity** – researchers need to make sure that they conducted their studies repeatedly across different times in order to ensure that the results are reflective of the current time period.

POINT -12 ASSESSING EXTERNAL VALIDITY

External validity can be assessed by:

(1) Replication in real-life settings: To test if the results of a laboratory experiment can be generalised to the real-world, the same methodology can be employed in a real-life setting (e.g. Mailgram replicated his obedience study in a run-down office). If similar results are achieved the research can be said to have high ecological validity (a type of external validity).

(2) Replication with different populations: To test if the results of a study on one sample of the population can be generalised to the rest of the population, the same methodology can be employed using a different sample (e.g. by studying a different cultural or subcultural group). If similar results are achieved the research can be said to have high population validity.

(3) Replication in the modern day: To test if results from an old study can be generalised to the modern day, the same methodology can be employed in the modern day (e.g. replicating Mailgram's 1960s study today). If similar results are achieved the research can be said to have high temporal validity.

POINT -13 ETHICS; INCLUDING THE ROLE OF THE BRITISH PSYCHOLOGICAL SOCIETY'S CODE OF ETHICS; ETHICAL ISSUES IN THE DESIGN AND CONDUCTING OF RESEARCH, DEALING

WITH ETHICAL ISSUES IN RESEARCH

Ethics

Ethical issues involve researchers assessing and acting upon all ethical considerations involved in research before it is conducted. The main consideration of the BPS is that the health and dignity of participants should be protected. The BPS – British Psychological Society has published a Code of Ethics that all psychologists have to abide by. Most research institutions (e.g. universities) have ethical committees which have to approve research projects before they take place. Before conducting research, researchers should also;

1. **Seek peer advice (from colleagues)**
2. **Consult likely participants for their views**
3. **Consider alternative research methodologies**
4. **Establish a cost-benefit analysis** of short-term and long-term consequences (from the participants point of view, distress and loss of time may be a cost however, this may be outweighed by the feeling that they have done something positive by contributing to psychological research. From the group to which the individual belongs point of view, when research is done to investigate cross-cultural differences, the research may not harm the individual however may bring about negative implications for the cultural group).
5. **Assume responsibility for the research.**

Exam Tip:

Avoid the mistake of confusing ethical guidelines with ethical issues.

- The guideline tells the researcher what they should do to conduct research that is ethically acceptable.
- An ethical issue occurs when there is a dilemma between what the researcher wants to do in order to conduct the research and the rights and dignity of the participant.

Ethical guidelines are standards of conduct or rules of behaviour set out by the British Psychological Society (BPS) adopted by various professions. Their aim is to help guide the behaviour of professionals. Psychologists are to use the guidelines to refer to when designing a piece of research.

Ethical issues – You need to know specifically about the ethical dilemmas that each of the following ethical issues can cause AND you must be able to set each one within the context of psychological research.

* Deception

* Informed consent (lack of)

* Protection from harm (lack of)

Ways in which Psychologists Deal with Ethical Issues:

- **Debriefing** – Revealing the true nature of the research once the participant has taken part – give the participant the option to withdraw their data.
- **Retrospective consent** – This is where the participant gives consent for their data to be used in the research once they've taken part and have been debriefed (know the true nature of the research).
- **Prior General Consent** – Asking participants to give consent for all potential research, once you have this they have technically given consent to be participants in any psychological research.
- **Presumptive Consent** – Asking a group that are representative of your participants, telling them the entire truth about the research and asking if they'd consent to taking part – if they do you can presume that your participants would also.
- **Confidentiality** – Ensuring that participants are not able to be identified. **For example, u**se initials (e.g. KF), assign numbers (e.g. Participant 32)
- **Right to Withdraw** – Ensuring that participants are informed (and reminded) about their right to withdraw themselves and/or their data from the research at any time.

Ethical Issue

Solution to the Ethical Issue

Lack of consent	Retrospective Consent	Prior General Consent	Presumptive Consent	Debriefing
Lack of protection of participants	Right to Withdraw	Keep information confidential	Termination	Debriefing
Lack of confidentiality	Don't use participant names	Don't share private information		

POINT -14 RELIABILITY

Reliability:

Reliability means **consistency.** The results of a research study are reliable if, when the study is replicated, the same results are consistently found.

This replication involves repeating a research study under exactly the **SAME CONDITIONS,** using exactly the **SAME PARTICIPANTS.**

Be aware: The results of an investigation may be reliable, but that does not mean that they are valid. A study can be reliably invalid (i.e. consistently produce inaccurate results).

Issues of Reliability (A Level Only)

Psychologists need to measure variables consistently. This aspect of research is known as reliability. If you are a reliable student you regularly turn up to your lessons and always hand in work on time. A reliable piece of research should always produce the same or similar results when replicated in exactly the same conditions with the same participants. Reliability is used to assess both experimental procedures and 'tools' such as tests, questionnaires, interviews and behavioural categories in observations.

Types of Reliability:

There are two types of reliability:

(1) Internal Reliability (the consistency of the measure within itself)

Internal reliability refers to the consistency of a measure within itself. Internal reliability refers to the consistency of a measure within itself. For example, the items on a questionnaire or questions in an interview should be testing the same thing.

(2) External Reliability (the consistency of a procedure from one occasion to another)

External reliability refers to the consistency of a procedure from one occasion to another. For example, an experiment performed on two different days, in different laboratories, or by different researchers should still produce similar results (e.g. two researchers using the same interview format, equipment, behavior schedule or test should obtain the same results).

Assessment of Reliability (A Level Only)

The two types of reliability can be tested separately to assess levels of internal reliability as well as levels of external reliability. Just because a test has high internal reliability does not therefore mean it will also have high external reliability. For this reason, it is worthwhile assessing both types.

Internal reliability can be assessed by:

1. Split-half reliability:

If you measure someone's IQ today you would expect to get a similar result if you used the same test to assess the same person in a few weeks' time. If the results were the same time (i.e. if the results were consistent, you could assume the test was reliable). Rather than waiting a few weeks to try the test again it is possible to use split test reliability. For example with an IQ test, split it in half give both halves to the participant and compare their score on each separate half. If scores on each half are similar psychologists assume the test to be reliable.

2. Equivalent forms reliability:

Two tests, questionnaires or structured interviews of the same type are given to the same participants. Participants' results on the two forms of the test should correlate strongly if the tests are reliable.

External reliability can be assessed by:

1. Test-retest reliability: Participants take the same test twice, at different times. If the results for the two occasions correlate, the test has high external reliability. This can identify individual items that generate inconsistent results or other factors that cause variation, such as different settings or researchers. This is typically used to test reliability of structured interviews or questionnaires.

2. Inter-rater/observer reliability: Two (or more) observers watch the same behavioural sequence (e.g. on video), equipped with the same behavioural categories (on a behavior schedule) to assess whether or not they achieve identical records. Although this is usually used for observations, a similar process can be used to assess the reliability of interviewers.

POINT -15 PSYCHOLOGICAL REPORT WRITING

Writing up Psychological Investigations

Through using this website, you have learned about, referred to, and evaluated research studies. These research studies are generally presented to the scientific community as a journal article. Most journal articles follow a standard format. This is similar to the way you may have written up experiments in other sciences.

In research report there are usually six sub-sections:

(1) **Abstract:** This is always written last because it is a very brief summary:

- Include a one sentence summary, giving the topic to be studied. This may include the hypothesis and some brief theoretical background research, for example the name of the researchers whose work you have replicated.
- Describe the participants, number used and how they were selected.
- Describe the method and design used and any questionnaires etc. you employed.
- State your major findings, which should include a mention of the statistics used the observed and critical values and whether or not your results were found to be significant, including the level of significance
- Briefly summarise what your study shows, the conclusion of your findings and any implications it may have. State whether the experimental or null hypothesis has been accepted/rejected.
- This should be around 150 words.

(2) Introduction:

This tells everyone why the study is being carried out and the commentary should form a 'funnel' of information. First, there is broad coverage of all the background research with appropriate evaluative comments: "Asch (1951) found...but Crutchfield (1955) showed..." Once the general research has been covered, the focus becomes much narrower finishing with the main researcher/research area you are hoping to support/refute. This then leads to the aims and hypothesis/hypotheses (i.e. experimental and null hypotheses) being stated.

(3) Method:

Method – this section is split into sub-sections:

(1) Design:

- What is the experimental method that has been used?
- Why?
- Experimental Design type – independent groups, repeated measures, matched pairs? Justify?
- What is the IV, DV? These should be operationalized.
- Any potential EVs?
- How will these EVs be overcome?
- Ethical issues? Strategies to overcome these ethical issues

(2) Participants:

- Who is the target population? – Age/socio-economic status, gender, etc.
- What sampling technique has been used? Why?
- Details of participants that have been used? Do they have certain characteristics
- How have participants been allocated to conditions

(3) Materials:

- Description of all equipment used and how to use it (essential for replication)
- Stimulus materials for participants should be in the appendix

(4) Procedure:

- This is a step-by-step guide of how the study was carried out – when, where, how
- Instructions to participants must be standardized to allow replication
- Lengthy sets of instructions and instructions to participants should be in the appendix

(4) Results:

This section contains:

- A summary of the data. All raw data and calculations are put in the appendix.
- This generally starts with a section of descriptive statistics measures of central tendency and dispersion.
- Summary tables, which should be clearly labeled and referred to in the text, e.g., "Table One shows that…" Graphical representations of the data must also be clear and properly labeled and referred to in the text, e.g., "It can be seen from Figure 1 that…"
- Once the summary statistics have been explained, there should be an analysis of the results of any inferential tests, including observed values, how these relate to the critical table value, significance level and whether the test was one- or two-tailed.
- This section finishes with the rejection or acceptance of the null hypothesis.

(5) Discussion:

This sounds like a repeat of the results section, but here you need to state what you've found in terms of psychology rather than in statistical terms, in particular relate your findings to your hypotheses. Mention the strength of your findings, for example were they significant and at what level. If your hypothesis was one tailed and your results have gone in the opposite direction this needs to be indicated. If you have any additional findings to report, other than those relating to the hypotheses then they too can be included.

All studies have flaws, so anything that went wrong or the limitations of the study are discussed together with suggestions for how it could be improved if it were to be repeated. Suggestions for alternative studies and future research are also explored. The discussion ends with a paragraph summing up what was found and assessing the implications of the study and any conclusions that can be drawn from it.

(6) Referencing (Harvard Referencing):

References should contain details of all the research covered in a psychological report. It is not sufficient to simply list the books used.

What you should do:

Look through your report and include a reference every researcher mentioned. A reference should include; the name of the researcher, the date the research was published, the title of the book/journal, where the book was published (or what journal the article was published in), the edition number of the book/volume of the journal article, the page numbers used.

Example: Paivio, A., Madigan, S.A. (1970). Noun imagery and frequency in paired-associate and free learning recall. Canadian Journal of Psychology. 24, pp353-361.

Other Rules – Make sure that the references are placed in alphabetical order.

Exam Tip: In the exam, the types of questions you could expect relating to report writing include; defining what information you would find in each section of the report, in addition, on the old specification, questions linked to report writing have included; writing up a method section, results section and designing a piece of research.

In addition, in the exam, you may get asked to write; a **consent form**, **debriefing sheet** or a set of **standardized instructions.**

Writing a Consent Form for a Psychological Report – Remember the mnemonic TAPCHIPS

Your consent form should include the following;

(1) **T**itle of the Project:

(2) **A**im of the study?

(3) **P**rocedure – What will I be asked to do if I take part?

You should give a brief description of what the participants will have to do if they decide to consent to take part in the study (i.e. complete a 15-minute memory test etc...)

(4) Will your data be kept **C**onfidential?

Explain how you will make sure that all personal details will be kept confidential.

(5) Do I **have** to take part?

Explain to the participant that they don't have to take part in the study, explain about their right to withdraw.

(6) **I**nformation? Where can I obtain further information if I need it?

Provide the participant with the contact details of the key researchers carrying out the study.

(7) **P**articipant responses to the following questions:

Have you received enough information about the study? YES/NO

Do you consent for your data to be used in this study and retained for use in other studies? YES/NO

Do you understand that you do not need to take part in the study and that you can; withdraw your participation at any time without reason or detriment? YES/NO

(8) **S**ignature from the participant and the researcher: will need to be acquired at the bottom of the consent form.

Writing a set of Standardized Instructions for a Psychological Investigation

When writing a set of standardized instructions, it is essential that you include:

1. Enough information to allow for replication of the study

2. You must write the instructions so that they can simply be read out by the researcher to the participants.

3. You should welcome the participants to the study.

4. Thank the participants for giving their consent to take part.

5. Explain to the participants what will happen in the study, what they will be expected to do (step by step), how long the task/specific parts of the task will take to complete.

6. Remind participants that they have the right to withdraw throughout the study.

7. Ask that participants at the end if they have any questions

8. Check that the participants are still happy to proceed with the study.

POINT -16 WRITING A DEBRIEFING FORM FOR A PSYCHOLOGICAL REPORT

This is the form that you should complete with your participants at the end of the study to ensure that they are happy with the way the study has been conducted, to explain to them the true nature of the study, to confirm consent and to give them the researcher's contact details in case they want to ask any further questions.

- **Thank** the participants for taking part in the study.
- **Outline the true aims** of the research (what were the participants expected to do? What happened in each of the different conditions?)
- Explain what you were **looking to find.**
- Explain **how the data will be used** now and in the future.
- **Remind** the participants that they have the **right to withdraw** now and after the study.
- **Thank** participants once **again** for taking part.
- Remind the participant of the **researcher(s) contact details.**

Designing Research

One of the questions that you may get asked in the exam is to design a piece of research. The best way to go about this is to include similar information to what you would when writing up the **method** section of a psychological report.

Things to Consider...

(1) Design:

- **What is the experimental method/non-experimental method will you use?** (Lab, field, natural experiment? Questionnaire (open/closed questions?), Interviews (structured, unstructured, semi-structured?), Observation).
- **Why?** (Does this method allow a great deal of control? Is it in a natural setting and would show behaviour reflective of real life? Would it allow participants to remain anonymous and therefore, they are more likely to tell the truth/act in a realistic way? Does the method avoid demand characteristics?)
- **Experimental Design type** (independent groups, repeated measures, matched pairs? Justify you choice?)

- **What is the IV, DV? These should be operationalized** (how are you going to measure these variables?)
- **Any potential EVs?** (Participant variables, experimenter effects, demand characteristics, situational variables?)
- **How will these EVs be overcome?** (Are you going to out some control mechanisms in place? Are you going to use standardized instructions? Double or single blind? Will the experimental design that you are using help to overcome EVs?)
- **Ethical issues?** (What are the potential ethical issues and what strategies are you going to use to overcome these ethical issues?)

(2) Participants:

- **Who is the target population?** – Age/socio-economic status, gender, etc.
- **What sampling technique has been used? Why?**
- **Details of participants that have been used? Do they have certain characteristics**
- **How have participants been allocated to conditions** (have you used random allocation? Why have you adopted this technique?

(3) Materials:

- **Description of all equipment used and how to use it (essential for replication)**

(4) Procedure:

- This is a step-by-step guide of how the study was carried out – from beginning to end, how are you going to carry out the study

POINT -17 QUANTITATIVE AND QUALITATIVE DATA: THE DISTINCTION BETWEEN

QUALITATIVE AND QUANTITATIVE DATA COLLECTION TECHNIQUES.

Data Types – Quantitative and Qualitative Data

Both qualitative and quantitative data are forms of empirical data-information which has been gathered from research observations.

Quantitative Data is data that is in numerical form (numbers and figures).

Evaluation of the use of Quantitative Data:

- **Advantages of Quantitative Data:** The data can easily be turned into a numerical value and is therefore easy to analyse.
- **Disadvantages of Quantitative Data:** The data is often limited to yes or no answers and rarely allows the participant to expand on their answers.

Qualitative Data is data that is in written form (usually response to a questionnaire – open question responses).

Evaluation of the use of Qualitative Data:

- **Advantages of qualitative data Advantages of quantitative data:** Qualitative data is an expression of feelings and emotions; therefore it generates a rich source of information that can be used to suggest further research.
- **Disadvantages of qualitative data Disadvantages of quantitative data:** It is more difficult to analyse than quantitative data and may need to be turned first into quantitative data in order to be analysed.

POINT -18 PRIMARY AND SECONDARY DATA,

INCLUDING META-ANALYSIS

Primary and Secondary Data

Primary data – information observed or collected directly from first-hand experience. Data that has been collected by the researcher for the study currently being undertaken, specifically relating to the aims and/or hypothesis of the study. Examples of primary data are the results of an experiment, answers from a questionnaire etc.

Evaluation –

(+) Researcher has control over the data; data collection can be designed specifically to the aim.

(-) Collecting primary data is lengthy and expensive.

Secondary data – information that was collected for a purpose other than the current one. Examples of secondary data are government statistics, results from another experiment by the same or different researcher etc.

Evaluation –

(+) Cheap to use, no need to set up data collection.

(-)Data might not exactly fit the needs of the study.

Meta-analysis

A statistical technique for combining the findings of several studies of a certain research area. No additional research is carried out, data from previously conducted research is collected and analysed.

POINT -19 DESCRIPTIVE STATISTICS: MEASURES OF CENTRAL TENDENCY (MEAN, MEDIAN AND MODE)

Quantitative Data Analysis – Measures of Central Tendency (Description)

When you carry out a psychological experiment, you end up with a great deal of RAW DATA, usually in the form of 2 sets of scores – one for each condition. The two sets of scores need to be compared to see if there is a noticeable difference between them. Often, you need to summarise this data so that you can easily see if your study has been successful.

A set of scores can be summarised by:-
1)   A measure of **central tendency** (or **average**) of the scores.
2)   A measure of the **dispersion** (or **spread**) of the scores. A measure of dispersion is a number which indicates how far each individual score (in the raw data set) is from the mean, (i.e. how far each score in the raw data set deviates from the mean).

There are **3 measures of central tendency:** the mean, median and mode.

1) MEAN – This is calculated by adding up all the scores in a group/ in the raw data set and dividing it by the number of participants. It can only be used when the data is at interval level.

For example: Imagine the following are scores from a memory test (out of 20) obtained from a group of teenagers (age 13 to 19 inclusive);

19, 18, 19, 20, 15, 16, 11, 14, 12, 19, 18, 19, 17, 12 (there are 14 participants in this research study)

In order to calculate the mean of these scores (the average memory performance of teenagers aged 13 to 19 in this study), we need to add all the above scores. This gives us a total of – 229

In order to calculate the mean, the total of the scores (229) needs to be divided by the number of participants in the study, which in this case is 14.

$229/14 = 16.4$, therefore, the **mean** memory performance in this study is **16.4**.

The Mean as a Measure of Central Tendency

Strength of using the Mean:

POINT: The mean can be considered an accurate and sensitive measure of the average of a set of scores.
EXAMPLE: For example, the mean takes all the scores in the data set into consideration.

ELABORATION: This is strength because, due to the fact that all the scores are taken into consideration, it can be seen that the mean is a highly representative measure of central tendency and therefore is an accurate representation of the whole data set.

Weakness of using the Mean:

POINT: A weakness of using the mean is that it can be influenced by rogue scores.

EXAMPLE: For example, in a set of data with similar scores (e.g. 13, 12, 11, 10 etc.) a score like 5 can be seen as a rogue score that will significantly lower the average (mean) calculation.
ELABOATION: This is a weakness because; rogue scores in the data set can significantly increase/ reduce the calculated mean score making it unreflective/unrepresentative of the raw data set.

2) MEDIAN this is the middle score. It is calculated by putting the scores in numerical order and finding the middle value. If there is an even number of scores, the two middle scores are averaged to find the median. It can only be used when the data is of at least ordinal level.

For example, in order to calculate the mean of the data below

19, 18, 19, 20, 15, 16, 11, 14, 12, 19, 18, 19, 17, 12 the scores are first arranged in ascending order,

11, 12, 12, 14, 15, 16, 17, 18, 18, 19, 19, 19, 19, 20 – now the middle **(median) value** of this data set can be established which, in this case is **17.5.**

The Median as a Measure of Central Tendency

Strength of using the Median:

1. **POINT:** strength of using the median is that it is unaffected by extreme, rogue scores.

    EXAMPLE: For example, the median is only concerned with the middle number in a set of raw data; it doesn't consider any of the other scores.

    ELABOATION: This is a strength because, only considering the middle score means that any other scores (in particular, rogue/extreme scores) are ignored, this makes the median more representative of the whole data set and therefore, the median can be said to be an accurate measure of central tendency.

Weakness of using the Median:

POINT: A weakness of using the median is that it doesn't take all the scores in the data set into consideration.

EXAMPLE: For example, the median is only concerned with the middle number in a set of raw data; it doesn't consider any of the other scores.

ELABOATION: This is a weakness because, only considering the middle score means that all other scores in the data set are ignored, from this, the accuracy of the median can be questioned – how can this be an accurate measure of central tendency if it doesn't take all the scores in the data set into consideration?

3) MODE - This is the most common score/the score that appears the most in a set of raw data. It can be used with any level of data, because it requires only at least nominal data.

For example, in the following set of data:

19, 18, 19, 20, 15, 16, 11, 14, 12, 19, 18, 19, 17, 12 the **mode** is **19.** This is because the number 19 appears more frequently than any other in this set of data.

The Mode as a Measure of Central Tendency

Strength of using the Mode:

POINT: strength of using the mode is that it is unaffected by extreme, rogue scores.

EXAMPLE: For example, the mode is only concerned with the most frequently occurring number in a set of raw data; it doesn't consider any of the other scores.

ELABOATION: This is a strength because, only considering the most frequently occurring number means that any other scores (in particular, rogue/extreme scores) are ignored, this makes the mode more representative of the whole data set and therefore, the mode can be said to be an accurate measure of central tendency.

Weakness of using the Mode:

POINT: A weakness of using the mode is that it doesn't take all the scores in the data set into consideration.

EXAMPLE: For example, the mode is only concerned with the most frequently occurring number in a set of raw data; it doesn't consider any of the other scores

ELABOATION: This is a weakness because, only considering the most frequently occurring score means that all other scores in the data set are ignored, from this, the accuracy of the mode can be questioned – how can this be an accurate measure of central tendency if it doesn't take all the scores in the data set into consideration?

POINT -20 SIGN TEST – INFERENTIAL STATISTICS

Quantitative Data Analysis – Sign test

A non-parametric test used for experiments where the data is at least nominal and repeated measures has been used.

Statistical analysis, like the sign test, produces an observed value, which is compared to a critical value (on a table of values) in order to determine whether a set of results are significant to a specific level.

Key Definitions:

(1) **Observed Value:** The result of the statistical test (in this case, the result of the sign test).

(2) **Critical Value:** The table result (in which you will compare the **observed value).**

Calculating the sign test

Let's suppose you want to find out whether students prefer a cooked or non-cooked breakfast (or neither).

You select 15 participants and complete the table below, if students prefer a non-cooked breakfast (cereal) put a -, if they prefer a cooked breakfast put a +.

P No	Type of breakfast	Direction
e.g. A	Cooked	+
e.g. B	Cereal	-
e.g. C	Neither	Omitted
1		
2		
3		
4		
5		
6		
7		
8		
9		
10		
Total		

To calculate the sign test; Insert the data into a table, use a plus or minus to indicate the direction of difference

1. To calculate the observed value add up the number of tallies for each option (+= -=) ignore scores of participants who have not selected one of the options (i.e. those who selected neither)

2. Add up the number of times the less frequent sign occurs (e.g. identify which column has the fewest tallies) – the total of the less frequent sign is the observed value (s)

3. Next, you need to get the critical value from the critical value table (this will be provided in the exam). To get the critical value from the table you will need the value of N (the number of participants (omitting any participants responding 'neither' or 'not with a '+' or '-'. In order to get the critical value from the table you will also need to know; the hypothesis type (one/two tailed) and the probability value.

4. In order for the's' value to be significant, you want the observed value (s) to be lower than the critical value (from the table). **Remember – the important 'r' rule:** When there is an 'r' in the name of the inferential test (e.g. spearman's rho) you want the observed value to be greater than the critical value (from the table).

Exam Tip – when writing up your results, use the **perfect paragraph** outline on the inferential statistics page on this website.

POINT -21 STATISTICAL (INFERENTIAL) TESTING

Inferential Statistics

We have all heard the phrase 'statistical tests' – for example in a newspaper report that claims 'statistical tests show that women are better at reading maps than men'. If we wanted to know if women are better at reading maps than men we could not possibly test all the men and all the women in the world, so we just test a small group of men and a small group of women. If we find the sample of women is indeed better with maps than the sample of men, then we infer that the same is true for all men and all women. However, it isn't quite as simple as that because we can only make such inferences using statistical (or inferential) tests. All statistical tests though are based on the idea of probability. So, before we start to look at the different statistical tests, we need to understand the role that probability plays in statistical testing as no test to guarantee human behaviour 100%.

Probability and Significance

We are all familiar with the notion of probability because we use it every day in the judgements we make about different situations.

Inferential statistics allow psychologists to make conclusions based on the probability that a particular pattern of results could have arisen by chance. If a study that found a sample of women were better at map reading than a sample of men had only arisen due to chance factors (i.e. how it happened to go on the day) rather than because a genuinely noticeable effect does exist, then it would not be correct to conclude women are better map readers than men. However, if it could not have arisen by chance or if it is extremely unlikely to have arisen by chance (e.g. because the difference between men and women was so large), then the pattern is described as significant.

Judging whether an effect is significant or not cannot be done just by looking at averages or other forms of descriptive analysis. Instead, inferential statistical tests must be carried out to ascertain whether results are significant (i.e. whether they are likely to have been down to chance or not).

'Chance' and 'Significance Level'

By 'chance', we simply mean a probability that we will 'risk'. You cannot be absolutely certain that an observed effect was definitely not down to chance no matter how strong the effect seems to be. However, you can state how certain you are. In general, psychologists use a probability ('p') $\leq$ 0.05, which means that there is less than or equal to a 5% probability the results did occur by chance. In other words, p $\leq$ 0.05 means there is at least a 5% probability that the results occurred even if there was no real effect present.

For example: Let's say that a psychologist wanted to investigate the effects of music on memory. They give their participants a memory test to complete without music and then a memory test to complete with music. The psychologist is hoping to find that the music (IV) will significantly decrease memory performance (the DV).

When carrying out the inferential test the psychologist is aware that there is no way that they can be 100% certain and conclude that the IV (music) will be the only variable to have an effect on the DV (memory) as there are many other factors that could have caused the music to have impaired participant memory (e.g. the style of music, the time of day, temperature of the room etc...) Although a psychologist will try to control for as many of these variables as they can, they can't be 100% sure that they have controlled for everything. It's like a Dr, they may carry out a blood test looking for diabetes, they may confirm that they are 99.9% sure that their patient doesn't have diabetes, but they would rarely confirm that they are 100% sure that they don't have diabetes as there is also a small possibility that the results are down to chance – i.e. the test may have been carried out in error at the lab etc...).

As a result, whenever a psychologist is carrying out research which leads to inferential testing, the psychologists has to make a decision how much of their findings they want to attribute to chance. As stated above, in most cases, psychologists use a probability value of 5%, this means that when drawing conclusions for a study the psychologist can report that they are 95% sure that the chance in the DV was down to the manipulation of the IV (so in the case of the example above, the psychologist would be 95% sure that it was the music that impaired participant memory performance, however, they are aware that there is a 5% probability that the change in the DV was as a result of something other than the manipulation of the DV – A **CHANCE FACTOR**).

In some studies, psychologists want to be more certain – such as when they are conducting a replication of previous research or considering the effects of a new drug on health (because here in particular we would want to be very careful about taking chances). In these situations, researchers use a more stringent probability such as $p \leq 0.01$, (here the psychologist would be 99% sure the IV had caused an effect in the DV but would attribute 1% that the change in the DV was down to another chance factor). In other situations, a more lenient level such as $p \leq 0.10$ might be used, such as when conducting research into a new topic. This chosen value of 'p' is called the significance level.

Probability values often used in research

$P<0.01$ (1% attributed to chance) – used when researchers are sure that the IV will have an effect on the DV (usually when a psychologist is replicating previous research where consistent findings have been obtained). This may also be used when psychologists are carrying out research in which the results need to be more or less guaranteed (e.g. when testing the effectiveness of a new drug).

$P<0.05$ (5% attributed to chance) – used in most pieces of research.

$P<0.10$ (10% attributed to chance) – used mainly when research hasn't been carried out before.

It is good practice in psychology that once a piece of research has been found to be significant at a higher level of chance (e.g. 10%) the research is then repeated under a lower level of chance (5%). The lower the value of chance, the more striking the psychological results.

Type 1 and Type 2 Errors

Although different levels of significance are used by psychologists, in general, most research does use $p \leq 0.05$. There are good reasons for using this 5% level.

(1) Type 1 Error: If you use a level of significance that is **too high (lenient)**, such as 10%   (or $p \leq 0.10$), then you may **reject** a **null hypothesis** that is **true.**

Consider this example… imagine someone takes a pregnancy test and it is positive, leading the person to accept the hypothesis that they are pregnant (thus rejecting the null hypothesis that they are not pregnant). What if the test was wrong and it was a false positive? This is called a Type 1 error – rejecting a null hypothesis that is true. In research, the likelihood of a type 1 error is increased if the significance level is too high (lenient) such as 10% (i.e. there is more probability that the results were down to chance and not the effects of the IV on the DV).

(2) Type 2 Error: A type 2 error is when a person is being too **stringent/harsh.** Psychologists may **reject** the **experimental hypothesis** and **accept** the **null hypothesis** when in actual fact they should be **accepting** the **experimental hypothesis** and rejecting the **null hypothesis.**

For example: If the result on the pregnancy test was negative even though the person was actually pregnant, the person would accept the null hypothesis that they are not pregnant when they are. This is a Type 2 error – accepting a null hypothesis that is in fact not true. In research, the likelihood of a **Type 2 error is increased if the significance level is too low (stringent) such as 1%.**

If you have...	...when, in truth, the null hypothesis is...	
	TRUE	FALSE
Rejected the null hypothesis	Type 1 error	Correct!
Accepted the null hypothesis	Correct!	Type 2 error!

So, what's the percentage probability of making a Type 1 error at the following significance levels?

$p \leq 0.01$ 1% chance that type 1 error has been made

$p \leq 0.05$ 5% chance that a type 1 error has been made

$p \leq 0.10$ 10% chance that a type 1 error has been made

Exam Tips:

(1) Remember, in your exam, if you get asked *'what is the chance that a type 1 error has occurred at the $p \leq 0.05$?'*Always check (if possible) to see if the results are significant at the more stringent $p \leq 0.01$, if the result is still significant at this level it is very unlikely (less than 1%) that a type 1 error has occurred.
(2) A type 1 error can never occur when you have accepted the null hypothesis and have rejected the experimental hypothesis.

Using Inferential Statistical Tests

Once you know about the level of significance you are going to use, you can decide which statistical test you are going to use to analyse your data to assess whether your findings are significant or not. Different statistical tests are used for different research methods, experimental designs and levels of measurement. There are seven statistical tests that you need to know about:

Non-Parametric Tests:

1. Spearman's Rho (or Rank)

2. Wilcoxon T

3. Mann-Whitney U

4. Chi-squared (or x2)

Parametric Tests:

5. Unrelated T-Test

6. Related T -Tests

7. Pearson's R

How do you choose which test to use?

This is simply based on the answers to 3 questions…

(1) Do I want to investigate **differences** or **relationships?** If your study was an **experiment** then you will be **investigating differences.** If your study was a **correlation** then you will be investigating **relationships.**

(2) What **sort of data** (or **levels of measurement**) do I have? (E.g. Nominal, Ordinal, Interval or Ratio).

There are several kinds of Quantitative data (or LEVELS OF MEASUREMENT) that you need to be aware of when deciding what statistical test to use in order to assess the significance of your data:-

Levels of Measurement (or Levels of Data):

(A) NOMINAL DATA: The researcher identifies categories of objects or behaviours and counts how many instances there are in each **category,** e.g., categories could be **"conforms" and "does not conform",** where the researcher would just count how many people fell into each category – they could produce a tally under each category. This is the simplest kind of quantitative data.

(B) ORDINAL DATA If data can be placed in rank order on a scale then it is ordinal data. Positions in a race provide an example of ordinal data. The runners are ranked according to their finishing positions- 1st, 2nd; 3rd.This data does not measure how far apart the items on the scale are since they are arbitrary. For example, they do not state the time difference between runners.

Any arbitrary scale is an example of ordinal data – measuring things like attractiveness, hunger, happiness etc… are all examples of ordinal data as there are no 'official' measures of these behaviours, i.e. these measures rely on personal interpretation of a scale.

(C) INTERVAL DATA: This is data that is placed on a scale, but the intervals are fixed e.g. time in seconds, height, temperature etc. This is the most precise form of data – the scales are **not arbitrary,** the scales are set and cannot be affected by personal interpretation (i.e. as long as someone can use a thermometer they should be able to give the same temperature reading of the same room at the same time of day as every other person).

(D) RATIO DATA: Similar to interval data but with the key difference that as well as being measured on a scale with fixed intervals, the scale has a true point zero. For example, weight or height are examples of ration data as they have a true point zero neither measurement can go below. Temperature on the other hand is an example of interval data as it is still measured on a scale with fixed intervals, but this time the measurement only has an arbitrary zero and the measurement can go below zero (e.g. -10 degrees Celsius).

And the final decision??

(3) What type of experimental design did I use?

Remember the **three** different experimental designs?

(a) Repeated Measures   (b) Independent Measures Design   (c)
Match Pairs Design

You may have noted above that the statistical tests were organised under **two headings,** parametric and non-parametric tests:

Parametric Test:

Parametric tests are better able to detect a significant effect. This is because they are calculated using the actual scores rather than the ranked scores.

However, this sensitivity can also be a problem if the data is inconsistent or erratic.

Criteria for **parametric tests**

- the tests should only be used on data of **interval/ratio status** – (ratio data is exactly the same as internal data only, it has a set point of '0' for example, measuring height would be ratio data (starts at 0), temperature would be internal data (the scores can fall below data, -1, -2 etc…)
- The data will come from a sample drawn from a **normally distributed** population (a set of data distributed so that the middle scores are the most frequent and extreme scores are least frequent).
- There is **homogeneity of variance** between conditions -the deviation of scores (measured by the range or standard deviation for example) is similar between populations).

Non-Parametric Tests:

- The tests should be of **ordinal level** (data that can be placed in rank order or is placed on an arbitrary scale).
- Data **doesn't have a normal distribution.**
- There isn't homogeneity of variance – the deviation of scores (measured by the range or standard deviation) **isn't similar** between populations.

Here's one way of remembering which statistical test goes with which answers:

Non-Parametric Tests:

When to use the Wilcoxon T test:

- The hypothesis predicts a *difference* between two sets of data.
- The two sets of data are pairs of scores from one person *(i.e. repeated measures design)* or related people *(i.e. matched participants design)*.
- The data are *ordinal*.

When to use the Chi-square ($\square^2$) test:

- The hypothesis predicts a *difference* between two sets of data.
- The sets of data must be *independent* (i.e. independent groups design)
- The data is **nominal**. Frequencies must not be percentages.

When to use the Mann-Whitney U test:

- The hypothesis predicts *difference* between sets of data.
- The sets of data are from different participants *(i.e. independent groups design)*.
- The data are *ordinal*.

When to use the Sign Test:

- **Difference** is predicted between two sets of data
- The data is at least **nominal level**
- A **repeated measures design** has been used

When to use Spearman's rank correlation (rho) test:

- The hypothesis predicts a *correlation*.
- The two sets of data are related.
- The data are *ordinal*.

Parametric Tests:

When to use the <u>Independent (unrelated)</u> T-Test:

- Difference is predicted between two sets of data
- The data is **normally distributed**
- An **Independent Groups Design** has been used
- The data is of **interval/ratio** level

When to use the <u>Repeated (related)</u> T-Test:

- Difference is predicted between two sets of data
- The data is **normally distributed**
- The data is at least **interval or ratio level**
- A **repeated measures or matched pairs design** has been used

When to use <u>Pearson's R</u> correlation (R) test:

- The hypothesis predicts a *correlation*.
- The two sets of data are related.
- Data is **normally distributed**
- The data are *ordinal* or *interval* (not nominal).
- The data are pairs of scores from the same person or event

A Diagram to Help:

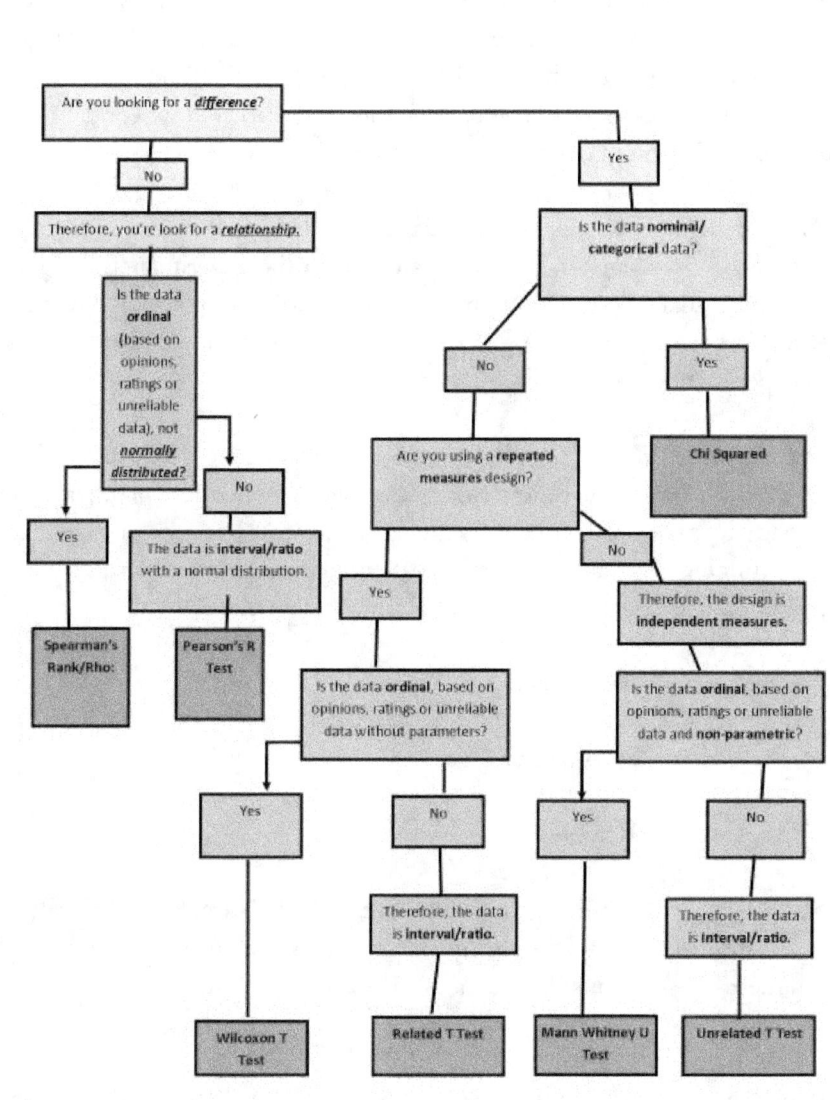

Justifying the Use of Statistical Tests

Exam Tip: This 'justify the use of statistical test' is a common question in the exam, you may be given a scenario/piece of research and would need to suggest what statistical test you would use (justify with the three categories that we have just mentioned above; (1) data/level of measurement, (2) experimental design, (3) stating whether the research is looking for a relationship between 2 variables or a difference).

When justifying your use of a particular statistical test, you need to explain why you chose that test. Base your answer on the experimental design and the level of data. If the question requires a third reason, add that it is a test of difference or it is a test of association (depending on whether it refers to an experiment or correlation).

For example, if you have conducted a study where you are seeking to determine whether there are differences between two independent groups of participants then you might state: In order to assess the significance of these findings it was necessary to use a statistical test. In this study an appropriate test would be a Mann-Whitney U test because

(1) The design was independent measures

(2) The data was at an ordinal level and

(3) A test of differences was required.

N: B you can also justify your use of statistical test by referring to **parametric and non-parametric** characteristics (e.g. you have used a parametric test because the data is normally distributed and uses interval data)

The Use of Inferential Analysis – Observed Values and Critical values

Each inferential test (Pearson's R, Related t-tests, Unrelated t-tests, Spearman's Rho, Wilcoxon T, Mann-Whitney U and Chi-squared) involves taking the quantitative data collected in a study and doing some arithmetical calculations which produce a single number called the test statistic.

The Observed Value: The observed value is always **the result** of the statistical test. For example, the result of the Spearman's Rho tests is the 'rho' value, the result of the Wilcoxon T test is the 'T' value, the result of the Chi Square test is the 'x^2' value, the result of the Mann Whitney U tests is the 'U' value, etc...

To decide if the observed value (your observed value/result) is significant, the observed is compared to another number, called the **critical value.** This number is not from your research but listed in **a table of critical values** (you do not need to learn these tables; they will be provided in the exam). The critical value is the value that a test statistic must reach in order for the null hypothesis to be rejected. There are different tables of critical values for each inferential test. To find the appropriate critical value in a table you need to know:

1, Degrees of freedom (DF) – In most cases you get this value by looking at the number of participants in the study (N). In studies using an independent groups design there are two values for N (one for each group of participants), called N1 and N2.

2, One-tailed or two-tailed test – If the hypothesis predicted at the beginning of the study was a **directional hypothesis**, then you use a **one-tailed test,** if it was **non-directional** then you use a **two-tailed test.**

3, Significance level – Selected, usually, at $p \leq 0.05$, $p<0.01$, $p<0.10$

Observed and Critical Values (and the importance of 'R')

Some inferential tests are **significant** when the **observed value** is **equal to or exceeds** the **critical value, for others it is the reverse** (the size of the difference between the two is irrelevant). You need to know which, and you will find it stated underneath each table. One way to remember which test requires the observed value to be higher than the critical value and which requires the opposite is by seeing if there is a letter 'R' in the name of the inferential test. If there is an 'R' (e.g. Spearman's, Chi-square, Pearson's R), then the observed value should be greater than the critical value. If there is no 'R' (e.g. Mann-Whitney and Wilcoxon), then the observed value should be less than the critical value.

Tests in which the observed value (the result) needs to be **greater** than the critical (table) value in order to be significant:	Tests in which the observed value (the result) needs to be **less** than the critical (table) value in order to be significant:
Spearmans Rho	Mann Whitney U
Related T-Test	Wilcoxon T
Unrelated T-Test	Sign Test
Chi Square	
Pearsons R	

Exam Tip: This is a Perfect Paragraph which would be useful to know for your exam when writing up whether results are significant or not).

Using the statistical test (insert the statistical test used), where the observed value of (R,T, rho etc.) is ___ (enter observed value) and the critical table value is ___ (enter critical table value) using a one/two tailed hypothesis the results can be seen to be significant/insignificant because the observed value is higher/lower than the table critical value where the P value is (enter P value) and the df are (enter df value(s) (i.e. number of participants used). As a result, the null/experimental hypothesis should be accepted and the null/experimental hypothesis rejected.

Chi Squared and Contingency Tables

What is a contingency table? A contingency table is essentially a display format used to analyse and record the relationship between two or more variables (it is used when we have categories of data).

Chi-Square can be used to investigate "differences" (an experiment), for example, a researcher may be interested to find out whether girls or boys are more aggressive and they may study this by observing girls and boys in a nursery situation (aged 3-4). The results gained can be analysed using Chi-Square to tell us whether there is a difference between these groups

Experimental hypothesis: There will be a significant difference in the number of aggressive acts performed by boys and girls in a nursery situation.

Chi – Square – worked example for a 2×2 contingency table (using the example given above).

A Chi-Square contingency table

	Girl	Boy	Totals
No. of aggressive incidents 0 - 5	Cell A 卌 = 5	Cell B 卌 卌 II = 12	= 17
No. of aggressive incidents 6 and over	Cell C 卌 卌 =10	Cell D 卌 IIII =9	=19
Totals =	15	21	= 36

POINT -23 QUALITATIVE DATA ANALYSIS

Qualitative Data Analysis and Interpretation

Many research methods such as naturalistic observations, open ended questions on questionnaires, unstructured interviews, and an analysis of participants' diaries or notes as part of a case study and so on, may generate qualitative data (i.e. data in written form). Although this data can appear very detailed and complicated, one way of simplifying this data to make it easier to analyse and interpret is by converting it into quantitative data.

One way of converting qualitative data into quantitative data is through a content analysis.

Content Analysis

Content analysis is a method of qualitative data analysis that involves rating or **coding** and categorising qualitative data. Rating systems are used to assess a wide range of qualitative data such as written or verbal observation records, questionnaire survey responses (where open-ended questions were employed) and interview content. The idea behind a **coding system** is to be able categorise occurrences of a particular theme, thereby converting the raw qualitative data into quantitative frequencies (i.e. a count is made of the number of times certain selected types of event happen).

The Procedure of Content Analysis

(2) A sample of **materials are gathered** (e.g. interview responses may need to be transcribed) and examined (i.e. by **reading the text through several times** until you know it well).

(3) **Key themes** are identified and these are used to create **categories** to help organise and classify the data- these categories will reflect the purpose of the research.

(4) **Instances** or examples of each theme occurring in the text are gathered and placed in the relevant categories.

(5) **Frequencies** can then be counted numerically for each of the different categories. The nominal data can then be quantitatively analysed with charts and graphs, measures of central tendency and dispersion produced and statistical analysis can be carried out.

(6) The researcher may then **draw conclusions** about human behaviour as a whole based on these findings.

A pilot study is often used as part of the analysis to generate and test the coding system to be employed. This helps make sure categories are exclusive and discrete (i.e. there is no overlap) and that all relevant themes are included and clearly operationalized.

Evaluation of using a Content Analysis:

(+) Strength of using a content analysis is that **Statistical procedures** become possible. When dealing with written/qualitative data it is not possible to use descriptive or inferential statistics. Converting qualitative data into quantitative data makes descriptive and inferential statistics possible which means that researchers are able to test for significance.

(+) Changing qualitative data into quantitative data makes the results more **objective.**

(-) Turning qualitative data into quantitative data can be seen to be **reductionist.** The complex and detailed qualitative data gets reduced to numerical figures which in turn reduce detailed/complex human behaviour to numbers and figures.

Although there are ways of converting qualitative data into quantitative data (such as content analysis), most qualitative researchers believe the traditional quantitative methods used by psychologists do not produce results that are applicable to everyday life. If a researcher is trying to produce numbers, then he or she is probably not engaged in qualitative analysis which is less concerned with counting responses or occurrences and more concerned with **interpreting the meaning of data** (i.e. quality rather than quantity). There are different ways of analysing qualitative data that preserve these principles and therefore do not aim to use numbers at all as part of the data analysis.

Thematic Analysis

This involves taking a body of text (qualitative data) such as a transcript of an interview or an observational record to analyse an existing theory, explanation or hypothesis (from the top-down). This involves organising the qualitative data into specific themes that were pre-identified by the existing theory. This allows the researcher to summarise the data gathered into distinct categories. This kind of analysis is sometimes also referred to as **'theoretical analysis'** as the theory and themes exist prior to analysis beginning. A similar process can be followed where there is no pre-existing theory and, instead, the themes or categories emerge from the data (from the bottom-up). This is referred to as **'inductive analysis'** or 'grounded theory' and helps provide new insights. Either way, the analysis follows a similar series of stages.

Stages in Thematic Analysis

(1) Transcribe the data if you need to, number each line and **read the text through several times** until you know it well. As you read the text, make notes of any ideas that occur to you.

(2) Divide the text into 'meaning units' using a forward slash (/) between every apparent change in meaning or subject.

(3) Search the entire text for meanings that seem to have a **similar theme and group these together.** You could highlight these using different colours.

(4) Keep adjusting the themes as you continue to sort through the data.

(5) Once you are satisfied that there are no more themes to find you will need to **define and name each theme** to form categories.

(6) These themes or categories can then be used to **draw conclusions** about trends in the data and what this seems to suggest about the area being studied.

A report is then written up whereby the researcher will need to present a case for each theme and provide some supporting quotations from the test

www.ingramcontent.com/pod-product-compliance
Lightning Source LLC
Chambersburg PA
CBHW062012280526
45787CB00005B/2070